TRIALS AND TRIUMPHS II

*Rooted and Grounded in Love:
Fifty Life-Changing Testimonies*

FAITHWRITERS

xulon PRESS

Handwritten note at top: Along with being head editor, I wrote Introduction and story on page 61.
Love,
Joann
(Jaci Smith's sister)

Copyright © 2015 by FaithWriters

Trials and Triumphs II
Rooted and Grounded in Love: Fifty Life-Changing Testimonies
by FaithWriters

Printed in the United States of America

ISBN 9781498416016

All rights reserved solely by the author. The author guarantees all contents are original and do not infringe upon the legal rights of any other person or work. No part of this book may be reproduced in any form without the permission of the author. The views expressed in this book are not necessarily those of the publisher.

Scripture quotations taken from the King James Version (KJV) – *public domain*

Scripture quotations taken from the New King James Version (NKJV). Copyright © 1982 by Thomas Nelson, Inc. Used by permission. All rights reserved.

Scripture quotations taken from the New International Version (NIV). Copyright © 1973, 1978, 1984, 2011 by International Bible Society. Used by permission. All rights reserved.

Scripture quotations taken from the English Standard Version (ESV). Copyright © 2001 by Crossway, a publishing ministry of Good News Publishers. Used by permission. All rights reserved.

Scripture quotations taken from the New Living Translation (NLT). Copyright © 1996, 2004, 2007 by Tyndale House Foundation. Used by permission. All rights reserved.

Scripture quotations taken from the New Century Version (NCV). Copyright © 2005 by Thomas Nelson, Inc. Used by permission. All rights reserved.

Scripture quotations taken from the Amplified Bible (AMP). Copyright © 1954, 1958, 1962, 1964, 1965, 1987 by The Lockman Foundation. Used by permission. All rights reserved.

www.xulonpress.com

Dear Tracy,

I hope you will enjoy reading this as much as I enjoyed being a part of it. There are so many stories in here that will encourage you and motivate you when you feel like giving up. Give your fears to Jesus as many times as it takes to leave them with him. Faith does not promise a trial-free life. Only through faith will you be able to triumph over this horrible trial, and when you do, Jesus, Jaci and I will do a happy dance! Mom always said, "Keep your chin up and your eyes on God." It used to drive me nuts, but now I repeat her wise words. I'm praying for you and your family.

Shann Holt

Table of Contents

INTRODUCTION ix

FAITH UNDER FIRE SECTION — Page

FAITH AROUND THE CAMPFIRE	By Dannie Hawley	15
A RENEWED MARRIAGE, A NEW SONG	By Abby Kelly	20
THROUGH THE DARKEST VALLEY	By P.J. Baker	25
RACHEL'S MIRACLES	By Jennifer Liang	30
THRIVING IN ADVERSITY: COMING TO THE END OF MYSELF	By Jaylin Palacio	34
PRISON BREAK – FREED FROM AN ONLINE CULT	By Amy Davey	37
HIS LOVE BREATHES LIFE ANEW	By CD Swanson	42
THE RIDE OF A LIFETIME	By Rebecca L. Real	47
TINGLES OF REASSURING JOY!	By Sandy Ott	52
DANCING WITH THE DEVIL	By Sheldon Bass	56
THREE CORDS	By Shann Hall-Lochmann VanBennekom	61
ASK AND YOU WILL RECEIVE	By Graham Keet	66
LIVING THE FAITH	By Edmond Ng	71
EMPTY	By Rachel Malcolm	73

A LESSON LEARNED FROM MY DEAD UNCLE	By Clyde Blakely	76
MY TESTIMONY	By Frances Seymour	81
FAITH IN THE FOG	By Carla Rogers	85
WHAT WAS I THINKING?	By LaVonne Wood	89
FACING DANGER, FINDING DELIVERANCE	By Trudy Newell	93
SO THAT	By Stacie Snell	98
PURPOSE IN THE PAIN	By Jeremiah Creason	102
ENDURING DREAMS	By Darlene Free Edmondson	106
LETTING GO	By Katherine Kane	110
MY JOURNEY THROUGH DEPRESSION	By Milly Born	114
ON BEING A PERSISTENT WIDOW	By Dee Hardy	118
CASTING BREAD UPON THE WATERS	By Mary Sue Moss	122
MOURNING INTO DANCING	By Julie Berry	126
THE WORST OF SINNERS ~ THE BEST OF GRACE AND MERCY	By Steve Bragg	130
HAUNTED BY HURRICANES	By D. Katy Tyler	134
TUESDAY AFTERNOON	By Dot Hannah	139

COMING TO FAITH SECTION

HE GIVES HIS BELOVED SLEEP	By Phyllis Sather	145
OUT OF THE BROKENNESS	By Maureen Hager	149
FINDING THE KING OF THE JEWS	By Sylvia Maltzman	154
FIGHTING THE GOOD FIGHT	By Lilly Grace	159
BEAUTY FOR ASHES	By Pamela Couvrette	163
I WAS A COVERT HELLION	By Linda Gage	167
IN MY CORNER	By Jules St. Jermaine	171
"GREG! WHAT WILL IT BE HEAVEN OR HELL?"	By Greg Mancini	175
ONE WOMAN'S TESTIMONY	By Sylvia Hensel	179

Table of Contents

RISING FROM THE ASHES, A QUEST OF REDEMPTION	By Robert S. Totman	183
FINDING THE ANSWER	By Kevin Ingram	187
THE LORD'S TERMS	By Sharon Eastman	191
HE HEARD MY PRAYER!	By Luella Campbell	195
ACCOUCHEMENT	By Cindy Maness	199
FIVE YEARS WITHOUT FEAR	By Lynn Gipson	203
NEW HOPE AND PURPOSE	By Maria Lee	206
GOD'S POWERFUL SAVING WORK IN MY LIFE	By Ken Grant	211
A BRAND NEW HEART	By Elizabeth Gordon	215
TWO-EDGED SWORD	By Richard McCaw	219
SOMETHING BEAUTIFUL, SOMETHING GOOD	By Tim Pickl	224
EPILOGUE	By Michael Edwards	227

INTRODUCTION
By Shann Hall-LochmannVanBennekom

In today's world, many people believe God does not speak directly to his children as he did in the Bible. However, the Scriptures are so much more than genealogy tracking and commandments; throughout both the Old and New Testaments, God speaks to you through his Word. He gives practical advice that still pertains to situations you may struggle with in today's world. The fifty authors in this anthology will show how they heard God speaking to them through the Bible, by hearing his voice, through another person, or even during a dream.

Each testimony demonstrates the many ways that God directly intervenes and reaches out to his children today. God loves you, and if you are willing to listen for his voice, he does indeed speak to you on a regular basis. You may hear God speaking to you as you read certain stories. Many stories include times when the authors weren't sure if God existed or cared about them anymore. Yet, God never gives up on anyone. By the end of the book, you'll realize how patiently and lovingly God dispelled the authors' doubts and fears. He wants to do the same for you as well.

In the "Faith under Fire" section, each author bravely shares his or her story, which clearly demonstrates the power and love of God. Whether the author was struggling with addiction, divorce, abuse, illness, or rape, God is the common denominator in each testimony. The authors reveal how God has changed them, healed them, or reintroduced himself to them. Even during the most difficult times in life, you will see how God speaks and interacts with his children.

The second section, "Coming to Faith," has many articles illustrating how God makes his presence known. Sometimes, God comes after the author cries out for help while other times, God actively seeks out his precious child.

The fifty amazing witnesses in this book will leave you wide-eyed, full of hope, and offer you the opportunity to develop a personal relationship with God. The thread that connects each of the stories together is God's love. After reading each article, I have no doubt that God not only speaks to me or sends me signs of his love, but also desires to reach out with this love to you too. He yearns to wrap his arms around you, no matter what has happened in the past.

As this book was coming together, Satan attacked many of the people working on it. I believe he was desperately trying to prevent us from publishing this book and making it available to people all over the world. However, God had other plans, and showed me His love after a particularly trying week. I had decided to distract myself by reading some of the amazing pieces found on FaithWriters.com. The following poem, "You Are Not Alone," by Verna Cole Mitchell, was the first piece I encountered. It is a great example of how God speaks to us and shows his love through other people. I hope it will touch your heart as well and prepare you to see God's love and hear his voice in the fifty amazing testimonies that make up this inspirational book.

You Are Not Alone

By Verna Cole Mitchell

God knows when you're misunderstood
When what you'd done was meant for good,
The words you should have left unsaid
And ones you wish you'd said instead,
The grief that weights you like a shroud
Till anguish makes you cry aloud,
The nights unending you're awake,
Concerned for which path you should take,
Your disappointment and dismay
When by a loved one you're betrayed,
The pains that come too great to bear
And moans you utter in despair,
The failing strength that weakens you
When there's more work you need to do,
The fear and worries that oppress
And doubts that leave you in distress,
The times you're tempted to give in
When Satan calls you into sin.

God understands your every care:
The heavy burdens that you bear,
Your weakness when you would be strong,
Your sorrow when you've done things wrong,
Your motives, buried deep inside,
The longed-for peace you'd have abide.

God's loved you from the very start.
He holds you always in His heart.
He blots out sin when you confess
And fills you with His righteousness.
He'll be your strength when you are weak

And bring to you the peace you seek.
He'll never leave you all alone
But love you always as His own.

ABOUT THE AUTHOR

Verna Cole Mitchell, long-time FaithWriters member, is blessed to be a daughter of God, as well as a wife, mother, and grandmother. A former English teacher, she has published four poetry books designed to inspire, to entertain, and to make the reader smile.

To see more of this author's work, go to http://faithwriters.com/testimonies2.ph

FAITH UNDER FIRE SECTION

FAITH AROUND THE CAMPFIRE
By Dannie Hawley

Just as my left foot moved forward and my right foot angled back, my grip on the weatherworn board faltered. Down came the heavy load onto the back of my ankle. Dragging the firewood to our campsite on the old slab of plywood should've been a real time-saver.

Fifteen-year-old Elaine and I had been laboring since early morning to prepare the ground for the high school girls' campsite. Stacking the firewood remained the only task.

I struggled to right myself. "Elaine, I can't twist enough to get good leverage. Please, set your side down and come help."

The teen yanked upward but couldn't get the slab to move. After emptying the board of all of the wood, Elaine tried again. She pulled, pushed, and twisted left and right. The splintery board simply wouldn't move.

Hearing my groans, Elaine's own brows furrowed. "I'm sorry; I don't want to hurt you, but I can't get this thing to move."

"Don't worry about it," I said, fighting to keep the tears from dropping. The pain reached a crescendo with Elaine's final pull. I cried out, but Elaine's shriek drowned out my own.

Following my young co-worker's gaze, I choked out a gasp. A dot of bright-red blood dripped from the rusty end of a stake-like four-inch nail.

Gingerly moving my injured limb, Elaine and I discovered a matching bright-red spot covering the hole atop my Achilles tendon. "Uh-huh. No wonder the board wouldn't budge. Well, it doesn't seem to be bleeding."

The intense pain produced when bearing weight on my damaged leg reduced my normal stride to a left-legged hop. When the wood had been stacked, one armload at a time, I hopped over to my car.

Turning to wave farewell to Elaine, I noticed her lips pressed tightly, her eyes narrowed. She needed reassuring. "Hey, don't worry. I'll be here in the morning."

Returning home began with the winding mountain descent. I performed a kind of one-legged ballet—left foot working both the accelerator and the brake pedal. Then, I clung to the wobbly handrail and hopped up the twenty-four rickety wooden steps to my apartment. Lastly, I crawled to the bedroom repeating, "All I need is a good night's sleep."

The rays of dawn streamed through the slit in my curtains, marking the end to my agonizing, sleepless night. Remembering my promise to Elaine, I struggled to the University Student Infirmary.

I exhaled as the physician gave up trying to move my ankle. "Your tests show extensive damage to the Achilles tendon; you need surgery."

"Okay, can you just give me crutches now? I'll come back on Monday; I promise. If I'm not on the mountain, they won't let the kids sleep outside."

The staff frowned when I started my hobbling descent of the steps. Each hip throbbed from the injections meant to relieve pain and prevent infection.

Shortly after, seated in my co-counselor's passenger seat, I regaled her with my story. Cathy said, "That's wonderful! It'll really build the girls' faith when they pray and the Lord heals your ankle."

Faith Around The Campfire

"But, Cathy, I don't really have the faith to believe God will heal my ankle when it can be fixed with surgery."

My reservations didn't dampen Cathy's enthusiasm. "That's okay; just let us pray for you. We'll have the faith."

Arriving at the mountain lodge, we located our little flock. "Welcome campers!" The director for this Fourth of July church event addressed the eager group. "The weather report looks like a big storm's headed our way. If you are amongst those who elected to toss your sleeping bags around a campfire, you might want to reconsider. There's room for everyone in the lodge."

The groans of our girls, indicating their disappointment, tugged at my heart. I turned to whisper, "No problem, girls. We can ask God to keep the storm from soaking us."

"We'll do that at the same time we ask Him to heal Dar's leg," Cathy added, as I cringed.

At day's end, our little band hiked over to the campsite Elaine and I had prepared for her classmates. With sleeping bags rolled out, the fire crackling, the time had come for the end-of-day prayers. I fervently pleaded with the Almighty Creator to keep us dry.

"Okay, girls, we've prayed for God to put His canopy over us all night," Cathy began. "Want to pray for God to heal Dar's leg?"

Clapping and "You bet we do," rang out all around our little circle of adolescents.

"But, God may not want to do it this way, you know. God is God, after all, and we need to let God heal me with surgery, if that's what He wants to do."

"Yeah, we know. But, you need to let Him heal you with a miracle, if that's the way God wants to do it, don't you?" said the youngest teen.

Kneeling all around my supine body, each girl laid one of her hands on my injured leg, praying with conviction that I would leap up in the morning and not need the crutches lying next to my sleeping bag.

Once the girls had settled in their bags, I fell asleep immediately, oblivious to the thunderous roar overhead.

As the incredibly cold mountain breeze of sunrise hit my face, I snuggled deeper into my sleeping bag. Then I remembered the kids. Wiggling back out, I focused on the pile of wood. I retrieved the needed pieces, and headed back to the campfire.

Squatting before the dying fire, I stoked the embers back to rising flames. Cathy's croaking early-morning voice startled me.

"Your crutches, Dar, you forgot your crutches."

Glancing back, I saw the lifeless metal crutches lying next to my sleeping bag. "Oh, I forgot." My voice was a scratchy whisper.

"God healed you! You forgot because you didn't need the crutches!"

Once Cathy's words registered, I dropped from my squat position. I sat on the cold ground and stretched out my right leg. I had no pain and easily rotated the ankle in every direction. Although the doctor had been unable to force any movement out of the ankle on Saturday, I awoke with a normally functioning ankle on Sunday.

When the assembly bell sounded, the girls sprinted to the lodge, eager to share the night's miracle. The morning's leader was speaking as we entered the lodge. "We are thankful that the cooks had the foresight to bring some wood in, away from the downpour."

"What downpour?" I whispered to Cathy, who raised her shoulders and eyebrows in response.

When the leader called for testimonies, the man whose campsite had been next to ours stood, shaking his head as he spoke, "Well, I lit out earlier to find my girl in Dar's campsite.

I know mine was a piece of flat mud, and so were a lot of others. I found theirs dry as a bone." Cheers erupted.

Our little band of jubilant campers rushed to the microphone, ready to share the exciting details of not one, but two miraculous answers to their campfire prayers.

Early Monday, the smiling infirmary nurse reached for the crutches. "Good thing you'll not need surgery," she said, watching my happy dance. "Not taking summer classes means *you'd* have to pay for it all, you know."

I froze mid-twirl. "No, I didn't, but I'm really glad God did."

ABOUT THE AUTHOR

Darlene Dannie Hawley attended college in Montana. After earning her Master's Degree in Nursing from the University of Virginia, she became a missionary, and currently, enjoys the role as Project Director of the Samaritan House Children's Center in the Republic of Guinea, West Africa.

To see more of this author's work, go to http://faithwriters.com/testimonies2.php

A RENEWED MARRIAGE, A NEW SONG
By Abby Kelly

Done, done, done. Leave, leave, leave. Not exactly the romantic words you want to apply to your marriage on a sultry, Saturday morning. But the mantra pounded through my mind as I stutter-stepped through the sea of happy people visiting the weekend farmer's market.

The one affectionate male in my life, my dog Brave, trotted ahead of me, straining his leash in search of dropped morsels or an admiring child. A fog hung invisibly over my head as if I could look out at the cute couples and families around me, but they couldn't't see me. They couldn't't see the tear tracks on my cheeks. They couldn't see my drooping expression. It wasn't their fault they couldn't see my pain; in the last six years, I'd gotten pretty good at hiding.

Done, done, done! Leaving, leaving, leaving!

I actually said those words out loud once. Just months before my husband's third deployment, I didn't think I could face another year of just wishing he'd stay gone. In truth, for all practical purposes, it felt like he was gone all the time—emotionally, mentally, romantically, relationally.

For six of ten years, my husband barely touched me. For six of ten years, I begged him for every half-hearted kiss. For six of ten years, he spent nearly every weekend living a fantasy life through video games. Finally, my heart hurt—Just. Too. Much.

Done, done, done! Leaving, leaving, leaving!

He said the words once. I had just become too demanding, he told me. It's just the way he was, and if I'd be happier somewhere else, then he'd disappear until I packed up and went home.

However, seven years later, on another sultry, Saturday morning, we still shared the same address.

I came home from the market and passed him slumped in the couch, thumbs twitching furiously. "Hey, Abby," he said.

"Hi." I had no more words.

Brave followed me to the master bedroom and bath. Slowly, I released my ponytail and stepped into the shower. It felt like moving through quicksand. My fight was gone. It was only noon. That left hours of a lonely Saturday afternoon to pass, while avoiding the annoying bleeps of his video game.

I turned the water on for one last scalding blast and then shut it off. My feet found the bleach-spotted rug. Quickly, I dried and went in search of my iPhone. Pandora radio was my best friend, a constant stream of encouraging melodies that drowned out the game sounds and whispered words of truth through the Christian station.

The very first song that Pandora selected was new to me. "Worn" by Ten Avenue North began with a mournful sound that resonated with my tattered heart.

The vocalist sang of a heavy heart and a crushing, invisible weight that made it hard to breathe. It seemed the voice was my own, my own story emanating from the tiny speakers. Of course, I've failed, and I'm not perfect, the melody went on wrenching confession from me along with anger. His hope was fading too; his soul crushed by unbearable burdens. I'm too tired, too worn to keep fighting.

My knees crumpled beneath me, leading me gently to the bedroom floor. *How could they know? How could they be singing the anthem of my heart?*

Kneeling, I buried my head in the quilt. Brave nuzzled close, seeming to intuit my neediness. The song went on, finally bursting with strains of longing, a soul-cry to God for redemption. When the final notes trailed off, the song didn't end on a happy note, but a hopeful one. It brought to mind David's words born of pain:

> "Why are you cast down, O my soul, and why are you in turmoil within me? Hope in God; for I shall again praise him, my salvation and my God." (Psalm 42:11)

Though light had not yet broken at the end of the tunnel, the psalmist and the singer reminded me that God is faithful and trustworthy even when I don't see Him working. Even when I'm tired and worn, I have hope because God is faithful. Even Hosea says it:

> "Let us know; let us press on to know the LORD; his going out is sure as the dawn; he will come to us as the showers, as the spring rains that water the earth." (Hosea 6:3)

The beautiful refrain of "Worn" wrenched a prayer from my long-silent lips. "Lord, I feel like I've prayed for our marriage for so long. I feel like I've tried to be obedient to you in all of it and to let go of my agendas and to serve my husband and God, but I'm simply out of words. I don't know what else to ask. But I know that you're a God of redemption. I need to know that you see me and that you will rescue me. Show me what to do."

I quickly bought the song on iTunes and played it over and over, letting the words wash my soul, speak my prayer and comfort me. God knew. He planned that song for just that moment just for me. My lungs seemed to re-inflate with the knowledge of my Father's intimacy.

Another year has passed. We're still married. Another long deployment looms before us. He's leaving for Liberia in two days, and I can't stop crying. "Oh God, I don't want him to leave!"

I stepped into the shower this morning begging the hot water to melt the crushing sadness from my shoulders. Fatigue clung to me; tears blended with the pulsing stream and slid down the drain at my heels.

Finally, I stepped from the shower, wrapped in the giant, blue bath towel monogrammed *His* and methodically prepared for the day. To do list: draft devotionals, edit Bible study, email agent, record video for vlog—all things that require a measure of joy in my salvation. I repeated to myself: *I must harness some measure of the complete joy Jesus came to bring me. I must set my mind on Jesus to find the perfect peace He promises.*

Still procrastinating, I checked my email one more time. There was an email from my parents' pastor's wife. She is aware of the previous years of agony in my marriage. She knows what God has done to redeem the years. In her closing lines, she offered some encouragement for the future.

"I'm thrilled that your marriage is at the place where you will miss each other."

New tears fell. It was true. What a glorious place to be! No longer do I wish that my husband would leave and never come home; God has given us a new marriage filled with oneness and soft hearts that will ache while we are separated.

I knelt in gratitude. The corners of my lips tipped upward; immediately joy fell over me like a mantle, and the pressure abated. A new song flooded my soul: *"Sing a new song to the LORD, for he has done wonderful deeds.*

*He has won a mighty victory by his power and holiness."
(Psalm 98:1 TLB)*

ABOUT THE AUTHOR

Abby Kelly is the author of *The Predatory Lies of Anorexia: A Survivor's Story*. She is the senior editor of *My Daily Armor* and maintains her personal blog. When she isn't writing, Abby and her dog Brave serve as a therapy team.

To see more of this author's work, go to http://faithwriters.com/testimonies2.php.

THROUGH THE DARKEST VALLEY
By P.J. Baker

One evening in June 2012, my parents visited. My husband hadn't slept for at least a week, yet had an abundance of energy. Usually polite and gentle-spirited, he ignored my parents and behaved aggressively over a small matter of preparing dinner.

For months, even years, the stress of owning a business had been increasing and now it was severely affecting his health. Besides these changes in his mood, I was seeing other worrying behaviours such as taking showers late at night, and laughing and talking to himself.

"I think he's going to lose it," I told my mum that night.

At 1 AM the following night, I was settling our baby after his night feed, when an almighty smash reverberated from downstairs. My stomach lurched. I prayed for bravery and crept down the stairs, to be greeted by a scene of chaos and destruction. I froze in the doorway; my brain processed one detail at a time.

The glass cabinet, shattered on the floor...

The dining table, in pieces...

The heavy wooden sofa, upturned across the kitchen floor...

The sight of my beloved husband pacing around, full of wild energy, in the midst of it all distressed me most. Whatever he was saying made no sense.

He'd lost his mind.

My heart was tight in my chest. I prayed for him in tongues; I desperately wanted God in this situation. He knew, even when I had no words.

Exhausted, he lay dead-still on the floor. I called the police, who came and took him to the nearest psychiatric hospital.

He was discharged from hospital a week later. Because there was no history of mental illness, no diagnosis or medication could be given. Instead, the doctors put it down to "just one of those things."

I was terrified and constantly on edge. My loving husband was now almost silent, icy cold, and dangerously unpredictable. From the first time he'd put his arm around me, he'd always been my safe person. Now, he was the main cause of my fear.

Like my aching heart, riddled with tiny pricks of pain, fragments of broken glass remained embedded in the carpet. Even after the broken furniture was removed, our home was a constant reminder of that dreadful night.

Each day, I woke up completely numb inside. From the moment it happened, I slipped into coping mode. I was on autopilot, going about each day while trying to ignore the heaviness in my soul. Depression pulled me under, while anxious thoughts raged unchallenged in my mind. All the while, my soul cried out, *Where was God when it happened? Where is God now?*

I couldn't hear or feel any answers. Yet, I was sure He hadn't given up on us. I couldn't comprehend a universe without a loving God at the centre, or imagine losing both my husband and my faith in God.

The prescribed medication numbed my heartache a little and helped me to function. My husband remained depressed and withdrawn, and refused to talk. I couldn't know what he was thinking. I feared the worst: he would hurt himself or leave us with no warning.

In February 2013, my husband's mood flipped from depressed to elated. Constantly talking excitedly about the future, the smallest piece of good news sent him into an upward spiral. He stayed up every night, finding tasks to keep him busy. I took our toddler and stayed at a friend's house for a couple of nights, hoping his mood would settle. But when we returned, he was even higher.

The following weekend, we'd planned to visit friends, a six-hour-drive away. His manic mood was causing him to drive recklessly. I was terrified that he would lose control and we could crash, but he refused to consider cancelling the trip.

Every night that week, I lay awake, worried about the impending trip to the point of feeling physically sick and my stomach tightening. I prayed, *Lord, may his mood stop before we leave for the weekend.*

On Friday morning, we packed and left. Within minutes, his driving mirrored his pace of thinking: one minute slow, the next racing ahead. He pulled over, unable to do anything but stand by the side of the road for a couple of hours. I took our child home on the bus, all the while whispering a shaky prayer, thanking God for saving our lives. *At least God still hears my prayers.*

By now, my husband's behaviour became increasingly bizarre. He was painfully aware he was ill and desperately needed to slow down, yet adamantly refused medical intervention. I called the hospital for help.

"There's nothing we can do, unless he chooses to come in."

"So I have to wait until he harms himself or someone else before you can take him in?"

The silence that followed spoke clearly: the law protects his human right to choose treatment. *But what about us?*

What is protecting our right to a safe home? I bit my lip and prayed for our continued protection.

That Sunday, friends noticed his heightened state of awareness, agitated mood, and inability to sit down. Later that night, he snapped again. He woke, muttering to himself and behaving very oddly. He didn't respond to me; his mind was elsewhere.

I called for medical help, and the police came and took him to the psychiatric hospital. The next morning, he was diagnosed with Bipolar I Disorder with psychotic episodes.

The diagnosis brought relief that our problems were being acknowledged, as well as help for my husband and me. He was prescribed medication and assigned a Community Psychiatric Nurse, who monitored his progress regularly. To help me cope, I was offered regular respite for our child. I started sleeping again, and every night, I thanked God for the help that would stabilise his mood swings.

However, due to the drugs' strong sedative effect, he took them erratically. His mood gradually changed from manic to depressed.

By September 2013, he became so depressed he stopped eating and showering. His nurse believed he was losing his grip on reality so readmitted him to hospital, where he was prescribed a different medication.

Although I felt guilty that his nurse and I arranged his hospitalisation behind his back, I was mainly relieved someone else was now making that decision. I felt surrounded by family, friends, and the church. This time, I didn't feel so alone.

Since then, we've both recovered gradually. Slowly, my numbness is shifting. Circumstances have made me acknowledge my fearfulness, anxiety, and stress. I've found meditating on the Scriptures enables me to trust God more. As my worry decreases, my confidence in Him increases, and I'm able to face challenges such as finally passing my driving test. Marriage counselling is helping us communicate again after a long period of silence.

At the time, I couldn't sense God with me. But looking back, I now see He was with us during the most difficult moments.

He protected us from physical harm during the storm.
He saved us from danger on the motorway.
He provided the right medical help at the right time.
He surrounded us with supportive, caring people.

Now, He is strengthening our marriage and taking away some of my habitual fear. I praise God because He walked beside me through the depths of this darkest valley and is now showing me the tiny trickle of hope that leads back to the sea.

ABOUT THE AUTHOR

P.J. Baker writes poems and short stories for children and adults. She enjoys teaching, singing, reading, and most of all, day dreaming. She lives in the most beautiful city in the UK, halfway between a mountain and a beach.

To see more of this author's work, go to http://faithwriters.com/testimonies2.php

RACHEL'S MIRACLES
By Jennifer Liang

"*Bie ku, bie ku.*" The tears flowed as the Chinese nurses tried to comfort me, a suffering American mother in a land far away. Just a few moments earlier, a seemingly routine nineteen-week ultrasound had ended tragically. The baby girl had died some weeks before, undetected.

I knew enough Mandarin to understand something was terribly wrong but not enough to follow the conversations discussing the fate of *my* baby. In the moment of my distress, nothing had been translated back to me. I was pushed aside to cry alone in the waiting area with my mind running 100 mph, each mile representing another probably far-fetched scenario of what I was dealing with. Even my Chinese doctor husband, Stephen, had temporarily abandoned me in his quest for answers.

When I finally heard the miscarriage diagnosis, my tears dried, and I was able to comfort a crying friend as she gave me a hug in my hospital bed two days later. Between my own crying spree and her hug, a major transformation had taken place in my attitude about the life and the death of an innocent child. While in my hospital bed, I read a book that provided me with a new life-changing understanding of Heaven and my daughter's place in it. To me, Rachel's death was more of a comfort than a life of pain and suffering for all of us.

To this day, I still have no idea why Rachel died, but I know beyond a shadow of a doubt that I will see her again in

Heaven. Our family has our own little greeting party waiting for the day we will join her.

I remember Rachel through the many miracles she provided along the way. Although most people would see this as a devastating situation, I'm thankful for the blessings I experienced during this time. Discovering that I would see her one day in Heaven was just one of the many ways God showed His faithfulness to me. Her story was one of continuous blessings and miracles that I believe were not coincidental.

On the day of my routine check-up, I was excited to see if we could learn the sex of our baby. After hearing the news that her heart had stopped beating some time before, it took me at least a day to recover from the shock. We were sent home and told to come back the next day to induce labor or have a D&C procedure. I anguished over what to do.

Deciding that it wasn't wise to make a major decision on an empty stomach, my husband and I found a place to eat. Over a simple Western-style lunch, we started to talk about life without our first child. While there, we saw the man whose apartment we'd planned on subletting in two weeks. He and his wife were leaving China earlier than intended, which meant that we could move into our new apartment in only two days. To be able to recover in a cleaner, brighter, more convenient apartment was a godsend. The rest of the day was spent arranging for time off from work and praying a lot with friends.

After a restless sleep, we went to the hospital the next morning. I'll never forget the events that transpired that day. For one thing, Wednesday, June 3, 2009, was the first and last time I saw my first daughter until the day I will join her in Heaven.

After attempting to induce labor via an injection, the doctor gave me medicine to take on an empty stomach. He told me my contractions should start, at the earliest, late afternoon, but most likely, they would start the following day.

As instructed, I waited for two hours in my room, and then I had the brilliant plan to have lunch at the restaurant next to the hospital. When I started leaking water along the way, I should have turned around and returned to the hospital. I was so hungry, however, that I convinced my husband, my nurse friend, and myself that everything was fine. Before I could eat more than one bite, I realized Rachel was on her way. She made her appearance into the world in the bathroom of the restaurant. I still can visualize the long, torturous walk back through the campus to my hospital bed. My husband supported me while carrying our tiny, bi-racial daughter's body in a tissue package.

A few friends visited me and brought flowers, gifts, and food. Since it was a fast delivery, I only spent one night in the hospital and was able to move into my new home the next day.

As a Caucasian foreigner living in China, I was very thankful for the fact that Rachel's birth was induced and not forced through a surgical procedure. My rare blood type and Rh factor made it difficult and expensive to find blood for emergency transfusions. Because of the Rh-negative factor, a visiting foreign doctor told me it was important to receive an Rh-immunoglobulin injection within seventy-two hours to prevent problems with future pregnancies. This medicine was not easy to find in China; we only succeeded after making six phone calls.

The first three hospitals we called told us they didn't carry the medication because their patients didn't need it.

Next, my husband contacted a Shanghai hospital who told him that they had the shot, but will only administer it there.

The fifth call was to a Beijing hospital. They informed us that I could get the injection, but it would cost one thousand US dollars.

Finally, on our sixth call, God answered our prayers. Because I had been seen at the Singapore OB/GYN clinic at six weeks gestation, they were able to prescribe the necessary medicine. They even knew someone who was travelling to our city and they asked her to bring it to me.

Three days later a Singaporean doctor friend brought it directly from the airport to my home and administered it while his two adorable girls watched. Even in southwest China, a hard-to-get shot was found and administered within ninety-six hours. It wasn't within the deadline, but better than not receiving it at all.

A year later, when I became pregnant again, we found out that it had indeed worked. One week after Abigail's birth, I participated in a pro-life remembrance of babies we had briefly known. The author of another book that touched me during my recovering arranged the event. She stressed the importance of naming and remembering children whom we barely knew. So far, Rachel has three younger siblings, only two of which are with us on Earth. Ectopic Sam joined her in Heaven in January 2012.

Rachel may have only lived for a short time, but her story continues to be an inspiration. Stephen and I choose to think of her as a blessing and a practical demonstration of God's faithfulness in any situation. We will always miss her, but know she is waiting joyfully for us in Heaven. Those who knew her will always remember her in this way, and those who didn't know her are encouraged through the telling of her story.

ABOUT THE AUTHOR

Jennifer Liang is wife to Stephen Liang and mother to a toddler boy and a preschool girl. She grew up in Hawaii and currently lives in New England. Jennifer is writing a novel about ideas from her years of teaching English in China.

To see more of this author's work, go to http://faithwriters.com/testimonies2.php

THRIVING IN ADVERSITY: COMING TO THE END OF MYSELF
By Jaylin Palacio

Everyone encounters trials and tribulations in life; the biggest challenge that I've faced took me completely by surprise. My husband of twenty years had an affair and left me alone with our children.

I did not have a career of my own, so I had no way of supporting myself. My husband and I were known to have a good marriage. I thought we were happy. I was so confused, and I had no idea what I was going to do next.

I clung to the only source of strength that I had...the Lord Jesus Christ, and He taught me so much during that time. In the midst of the chaos, He gave me glimpses of peace. Even when I couldn't feel His presence, He helped me realize that God worked on my behalf. He didn't need me to do a single thing. He wasn't surprised when I went through this horrendous time in my life. It didn't catch Him off guard.

Yet, I found myself feeling frightened...doubting... worrying about the future. I heard Him say, *Why are you so afraid? Do you still have no faith?*

During that time in my life, I learned to control what is in my power to control. I can control my feelings, my words, and my choices. Also, I learned to put into the "God Box" all the stuff I cannot control, such as what others say, feel, or do.

I thought of Jesus facing the ultimate betrayal. As He was being whipped, insulted, and spat upon, He didn't speak a word. That is Divine Power. He did not react to the circumstances. Perfect silence. Perfect self-control.

As much as I tried to wrap my mind around what I was going through and question why it happened to me, I found that I needed to release it to God. I knew He would unravel the puzzles of life. God taught and corrected me. I was secure in the knowledge that He is able to set right everything that is wrong.

Isaiah 40 reminded me that the Word of God stands forever. People die away. Why did I worry about what my soon-to-be-ex-husband said about me, or why he and his girlfriend betrayed me so badly? In the big picture, none of that mattered. All of this will wither and fade, but the Word of God stands forever (Isaiah 40:8).

The thought of raising two teenagers by myself was incredibly daunting. I wondered how I would ever accomplish such a task. Then I realized that God would gently lead me. There is no one above Him. Who was better qualified than He to advise me in raising my children? How could I say that the Lord had not seen my troubles? He is all knowing. He never grows faint or weary. No one can measure the depths of His understanding (Isaiah 40:28). I discovered that when I didn't know how to be a good parent and I was completely worn out, I could turn to Him.

The Lord gives power to those who are tired and worn out. He offers strength to the weak (Isaiah 40:29). During that time, I was under the most stress that I had ever experienced. Daily tension headaches started from the time I woke up in the morning, and they did not go away. The weight of having to make huge decisions about the future and not being prepared to be a single parent seemed unbearable. I was tired all the time, and my mind was constantly filled with worry about all the decisions that had to be made. Nevertheless, I learned a valuable lesson. *"But those who wait on the Lord will find new strength. They will fly high on wings like eagles. They will run and not grow weary. They will walk and not faint."* (Isaiah 40:31 NLT)

I came to a place where my humanity, my limited emotional and physical strength, ended. I had run out of personal resources. It was the end of myself. I was completely spent, and I had no choice but to call out to God; and He was faithful to answer.

The song, "Hold On" by 33 Miles, touched my heart because it is the very message that God gave me as I endured this trial. My heart ached beyond belief, as I struggled to get through each day. During the darkest times, God whispered in my ear. I know you hurt, my precious child, but I am here for you. I understand what pain and betrayal feels like, and you can lean on me.

I was able to thrive in the midst of adversity because I held on to God. When I found myself at the end, with no other resources, I completely relied on Him. He knew exactly what I needed and was working on my behalf. I needed to do my job, trust in Him, and I was able to rest in knowing that He was really the one in control.

ABOUT THE AUTHOR

Jaylin Palacio is the author of He Will Never Leave You, a book about the devastation of infidelity, the faithfulness of God, and the healing power of forgiveness. A recent empty nester, she lives with her husband in Oregon, USA. She offers weekly email messages to help ease the pain of infidelity.

To see more of this author's work, go to http://faithwriters.com/testimonies2.php

PRISON BREAK – FREED FROM AN ONLINE CULT
By Amy Davey

My heart is beating rapidly in my throat as I awake on the hard ground, and I'm constrained in a sweaty sleeping bag. I shoot straight up, looking around to get my bearings. My husband is sound asleep beside me, blissfully unaware of the torturous dream I've just escaped. I sit perfectly still and remind myself that I'm safe now. No one is going to get me; only my family knows where I am.

My breathing slowly returns to normal as reality settles in. Still too frightened to sleep in case the vengeful man from my dream would catch me, I decide to get up and go for a walk.

Our two young children sleep peacefully on the opposite side of the tent, and for a moment, I admire their innocence. My daughter's blonde hair half covers her face, and she's lying sprawled in a comical position. She's only six years old, but has already lived through more than any child should have to. My son is curled in a ball beside her, his blond curls swept behind his ear showing his pudgy baby cheeks. At two, he's blessedly unaware of the recent events of our lives, and for that, I'm grateful. I slip out of the sleeping bag and quietly unzip our family tent, careful not to wake them.

As I step out into the brisk morning air, the dew clings heavily to every tree branch and blade of grass. It soaks the ground for a fresh new day. I wander aimlessly through the campground on this early August morning. Very few are awake. *How odd that after exiting a cult the world can be such a terrifying place, and still be so breathtakingly beautiful.*

I return to our campsite and settle onto the bench of the damp picnic table, standard with every site. I pull out the new journal I received as a gift from my parents at the end of the three-day intervention. As I begin to write, my fears immediately begin to subside.

August 21, 2010

Dear Diary,

Today is my first day free from the Trumpet Call of God cult; I feel more scared and shameful than happy. Am I making the right decision? I think I am; they're liars.
God loves me still, I'm pretty sure anyway. What if I'm wrong? What if he punishes me for leaving? Will they come after me?
Please Lord; let me know you still love me. The last three days seem like the longest of my life, captive in my parents' house with a Cult-Intervention Specialist. I'm grateful not to have to return to work quite yet. I can't believe they actually hired a professional from out of country, and even took my keys and cellphone to keep me from contacting the leaders or running away.

I close the journal and join my family—mom and dad, husband and kids—now gathering around the campground fire pit. They think I could use a break, and I'll admit they're right. I shake my head in disbelief and shame.

As we sit by the fire chatting, I feel a bit like an alien in a foreign country. *I don't fit in anywhere anymore.* I obviously don't fit in with the Trumpet Call of God members, who had been closer than family for the past several months; and I don't even feel normal with my real family yet, a bit like a goldfish in a bowl, I figure.

At that moment, my dad takes his seat by the fire, and I notice a small package tucked under his arm. He holds it out, and I recognize the packaging immediately. Freezing, I feel my heart jump into my throat again; it's the box of cards meant to spread their propaganda, but why does Dad have them?

"I thought you might want to burn these in the campfire." He looks expectant.

Not saying anything for a moment, I let what he's asking me sink in. He wants me to burn the ties to the cult by burning the cards. It still feels somewhat wrong—like burning pictures of an old boyfriend, but if I refuse, they'll think I'm still under cult influence, so I take the box.

I slowly pull small handfuls at a time out of the box and toss them into the fire. We all watch as their edges curl under the intense heat and flame. Silently, I say goodbye once and for all, no more Trumpet Call of God for me, on to life again—whatever that looks like in the aftermath. Former Cult Member. That label is surreal. They say former cult members sometimes become cynical about faith, choosing to abandon spirituality altogether. Not me, I decide. I'll admit this road has been a scary one, but Jesus rescued me in spite of my mistakes. I'll always follow him.

When I finally return home, the house I walk into is somehow different from when I left it more than a week ago. Still rather spooked, I delete my contacts with the members in the cult, and though I know this isn't the end of the battle in my mind and heart, I know I can trust Jesus to heal that, too.

Trials and Triumphs II

As time passes, I slowly cross each hurdle, re-integrating with my family, community, and eventually the church. I decide to write a poem as I reflect on what happened.

Here I stand at the edge of the cliff, do I jump?
You hold my hand and we leap together.
Falling is like flying, and in your arms is bliss.
You show me the world and all the
wonderfulness you made.
I don't know why I didn't see it before;
was it there all the time?
You gently place a pearl necklace around
my neck with care,
and you call me your own and tell me
your kingdom is mine.
I am your princess bride, your daughter, your love.
As I watch your face, suddenly the clouds blow in
as if from nowhere,
dark and menacing.
I look to you, and you smile. You take my hand as
we walk through the storm.
Winds blow, and the rain is stinging my face,
but the pain doesn't last with you here.
My hand slips from yours momentarily, and I fall,
swept up in the giant waves.
I scream inside my mind afraid that you are gone.
How will you ever find me beneath the swelling sea?
I choke and flail.
All around me the water batters my body,
unrelenting and cold.
You're gone; how could you let me fall? You had to have
known I would; why didn't you stop it?
A voice whispers through my fear, "I'm here."
"Where are you?" I cry.
I turn, and there you are. You never left my side.

You pull me from the surging waters and wrap your arms
around me tightly.
The fear is gone; nothing can hurt me when I'm yours.
And you will always be,
my Love.

ABOUT THE AUTHOR

Amy Davey is a Christian freelance novelist, poet, and blog writer. She has written several articles for online publications. Amy lives with her husband and two children in Port Hope, Ontario, Canada.

To see more of this author's work, go to http://faithwriters.com/testimonies2.php.

HIS LOVE BREATHES LIFE ANEW
By CD Swanson

I always knew about Jesus and revered the Lord. However, I can honestly say it wasn't a true connection in my younger days. It was more of an *affiliation* with the Lord, not a complete commitment and certainly lacking in intimacy. I truly suspected there was more, but didn't realize the full spectrum of how He operated, nor the capacity in which He loved. I wouldn't realize the depth of that love until a little later in life.

Throughout my school days, I was quiet and completely into reading and writing, which brought a sense of peace to my life. I always had a hand raised, eager to answer. I was the kid who'd remind the teacher, "You forgot our homework assignment," to a cacophony of moans and groans. Needless to say, I was hardly popular due to my appetite for acquiring a higher level of knowledge.

I basically lived for school. I could hardly wait to get up in the morning for another day of learning. However, things started happening that began to affect my mind and spirit. I was bullied and emotionally abused repeatedly. One of my teachers would yell, "Put your hand down, no one wants to hear what you have to say!" Eventually, I stopped raising my hand, and began to feel anything I had to say was worthless.

The emotional abuse continued to escalate. My peers made fun of me. They'd break into little groups, deliberately excluding me. I began to dislike going to school. I'd come home and read. My *world* was all about reading and writing. I cried a lot and believed I was worthless. My parents—both loving and kind—didn't know about the abuse. I didn't want to worry them. I began to self-isolate.

The bullying worsened in Junior High. I was pushed around and targeted by individuals who took great delight in messing with me mentally and physically. They'd mimic and call me names, as I'd walk by. Again, I didn't tell anyone about what was happening, somehow believing it was my fault, and that something was wrong with me. Until one particularly grim day that would change *everything* in dramatic fashion.

I was washing my hands in the ladies' bathroom when the late bell sounded. I gathered my books and rushed out into the corridor. I was mentally preparing for the history test I was about to take and quickened my pace. The class was within sight when I felt a paralyzing pain jolt through my spine. Before I had realized what had happened, four girls surrounded me. They grabbed hold of both arms, and held me, while the biggest, heaviest one punched me over and over. It seemed an eternity elapsed before they had stopped— I was pushed down onto the cold marble tiles—I tasted blood, and heard fiendish laughter before mercifully, everything went black.

I opened my eyes and heard the nurse asking, "Do you know where you are?" I looked at the blood on my dress through swollen eyes. I wanted to pull my head off to stop the excruciating and nauseating pain.

I began to cry, "I want Daddy! Call Daddy!"

I was so traumatized after that horrific incident that I became withdrawn, and no longer wanted to attend school. I became overly fearful and acutely conscious of my external stimuli. I had emotional scars and diagnosed with acute trauma collapse.

After numerous consultations with the school board and a Christian youth counselor, it was determined that I could stay at home to finish out my year. I had difficulty concentrating at first. My parents were patient, understanding, and loving during my entire ordeal. And, they worked dutifully with me, and my teacher's suggestions.

While being home-schooled, I felt Jesus *stronger than ever*. He was knocking on my heart, begging me to let Him in *deeper*. His love was like none other. I began to realize that, whereas my teacher in grade school didn't want to hear anything I had to say, *Jesus did*. I realized that, although the students made fun of me and ostracized me, *Jesus loved me unconditionally*. I began to heal, physically and emotionally, each day becoming stronger. I thrived in my studies at home. While being counseled weekly, along with my understanding parents' love and acceptance—and most especially with Jesus in my life—I healed.

At the end of the term, I was faced with a predicament: I could return to classes the following semester or remain at home for the final year of middle school. I struggled with feelings that were convoluted and conflicted all at once. I had wanted to attend school again. Yet, I was reticent about a return and the possibility of additional bullies repeating what I had already endured.

Prayers and the love of our Lord helped me. God gave me the courage and fortitude to return the following school term. That experience helped shape my life, and prepared me for my adult years. I sincerely longed to help others, especially those bullied or abused.

I'd learned more about the individuals who hurt me. They were random girls, who were outcasts and juvenile delinquents. They had sneaked into the building looking for trouble. They were sent to reform school after that incident. Being late for class that day was the only reason I was

His Love Breathes Life Anew

attacked. Apparently, I wasn't the only victim of their cruel games. It turned out they had prior records.

I am glad they were stopped before doing irreparable harm to others. I thank the Lord for His loving hand in all of this. I began to pray for them, and hoped they would find Christ and peace in their lives. I forgave them. That was the best thing about accepting Jesus Christ in my life—His love taught me to forgive and move forward in peace (Matthew 6:14-15).

Looking back, I realized that God turned my ashes into beauty (Isaiah 61:3). I didn't know it, but during my days of emotional and physical abuse, my career was being formed. I began to want to help people. I wanted to become a "voice" for those who needed guidance. God laid this upon my heart and gave me my calling.

I went into social services, and became an advocate for the elderly. I worked in the nursing home/assisted living industry my entire career, becoming an active participant in thwarting abuse of the elderly in the community. I loved every single moment of it. I became a director, where I was able to be their "light" and "protector" through Jesus Christ.

And it all started with Jesus knocking on my heart, wanting me to accept Him on an intimate basis. I'm so blessed and so happy that I opened my heart that day. His love made me fully realize what life is all about. Amen.

"Behold, I stand at the door, and knock: if any man hear my voice, and open the door, I will come in to him, and will sup with him, and he with me." (Revelation 3:20 KJV)

ABOUT THE AUTHOR

CD Swanson loves God and writes for His glory. To date, she has sixteen Christian books published. She has a devotional website ministry and contributes to various magazines and websites. Married to her childhood sweetheart, they share their home with their "furry boy" in the USA.

To see more of this author's work, go to http://faithwriters.com/testimonies2.php

THE RIDE OF A LIFETIME
By Rebecca L. Real

My husband Kevin and I were married in 1980. He called me his anchor because I kept him grounded in faith and steady in life. I called him my gift from God because I believed he was the answer to my life-long prayers for a loving, family-oriented, God-fearing husband.

We raised our family, grew deeper in love every year, and lived a pretty normal life. However, in September 2006 after discovering a lump where it didn't belong, Kevin was diagnosed with an aggressive and terminal form of leukemia. With that news, we lost our normal life and began our seven-and-a-half-year battle with the demon *cancer*.

Using everything in their arsenals, doctors smashed into the disease. Kev endured six months of powerful chemo cocktails that dripped into his veins and attacked the cells that had settled into his bone marrow, lymph nodes and blood. The first treatment gave us four years of remission and life almost felt normal again, despite the bi-monthly oncology appointments to track the monster's sleep.

In 2011, the beast awoke, and we once again marched into war. This time, the treatments couldn't hold back the demon, and the attacks on his body created a slow-but-steady decline. For nearly three more years, we faced our battles encased in God's armor and with our family and faith community marching with us.

Along the way, we didn't always make the right choices. We missed opportunities. We were afraid and uncertain. But most importantly, we held hands, laughed, cried, prayed, shared life, celebrated, made memories, and were blessed. Our once-normal life felt like a wild, twisted carnival ride.

Early November 2013, Kevin was admitted into the Critical Care Unit of the hospital. Despite his warrior spirit, his body had begun to fail. I brought him home under hospice care on December 3rd. On December 7th at 4:30 AM, he died.

He had been an early riser, so it seemed fitting that he'd be lifted into Heaven in the early-morning hours. Holding his hand, I sat beside him, tears streaming down my cheeks as his lungs breathed their last air, and his heart gently ceased to beat. I was spellbound by the changes in my husband's face. Deep wrinkles of pain that had crossed his forehead were erased as though a hand gently wiped them away. His teeth unclenched, and the corners of his lips tipped up ever so slightly into a soft-and-peaceful smile. His complexion transformed from a sallow yellow-gray to a light pink with two soft rosy patches across his cheeks. His face radiated peace and beauty. I witnessed a miracle as he finally and completely was healed.

Now I'm on a new journey. Despite more than seven years of advanced notice, there is no way to prepare for the roller coaster of grief. At times, the pain of losing him smashes into my very being and knocks me to my knees. It wraps itself around me like steel bands in a coiled spring, and I can't catch my breath. Memories flit through my head, and I laugh, sob, or am stunned into silence. I am broken and wonder if the shattered pieces will ever come together again.

Yet in the midst of this stormy ride, I can choose how to respond. It would be easy to curl up into a ball and grip the familiar pain around me like a blanket. It would be easy to become—and stay—angry. It would be easy to close my eyes and scream until I have no voice left. It would be easy to believe I am alone. It would be easy to believe that I will never again laugh, feel love, dance, or experience joy.

But I can't do that. God loves me and gave me the gift of over thirty-three years of life with my husband. His death can't destroy me. *Life*—ours in marriage and now mine alone—has to mean something more.

I'll say it again: *I can't do that.* Instead, I am gripping onto God's promises with both hands and storing them in my heart:

> *"Have I not commanded you? Be strong and courageous. Do not be afraid; do not be discouraged, for the Lord your God will be with you wherever you go." (Joshua 1:9 NIV)*

> *"I pray that God, the source of hope, will fill you completely with joy and peace because you trust in him. Then you will overflow with confident hope through the power of the Holy Spirit." (Romans 15:13 NLT)*

> *"For I know the plans I have for you, declares the* LORD, *plans to prosper you and not to harm you, plans to give you hope and a future." (Jeremiah 29:11 NIV)*

In the midst of a ride I didn't want to take, after fighting a battle I didn't expect, and accepting an outcome I didn't want, I choose to pray, to worship, to connect with others, to reach out to God. I choose to be vulnerable, honest, and open to His blessings in my life. I choose to see God in the smiles, hugs, tears, and warmth of those who love me. Our God is good. I choose to live in hope and "Ride the Ride."

Ride the Ride
Lord, I'm left with questions:
What's an anchor without something to hold?

What's a gift when it's taken away?
What is my purpose, and how does life's meaning unfold?
When death crashes in and steals life away, how do I keep going, day after day?

At first there is numbness and distance from pain.
Activities, people, cards, food and sympathy come pouring in.
Then time marches forward, and outreach declines.

I want to be normal.
I put on a face.
But the numbness wears off, and reality strikes.

He's not coming back.
That's not going to change.

There's a hole in my heart.
Pain smashes in.
It shrieks, and it screams and tries to tear me apart.

The roller-coaster ride that I find myself on is filled with lows, loops and drop-offs.
It startles and scares me, shaking my soul.

I try to hold on.
I want it to stop.
I grab onto the side and the bar in the front.
My knuckles are white from how tightly I grip.

When questions are asked, and pain is released,
In moments of silence,
In places of grace,
God gently gives answers,
So simple and kind:

An anchor has meaning because of where it is **placed**—not only because of what (or who) it holds.
A gift draws meaning from the **act of giving**—not only as a gift.
My purpose and meaning will unfold as I **live**.
I will keep going—moment by moment—because I have **purpose**, I am **loved**, and I am **not alone**.

Now, because I hold these answers deep in my heart, I choose to:

Place my trust in God.
Ride the ride.
Let go of the pain.
Allow tears to stream.
Cry out God's name.

Look out around—into time, into space.
See gifts He has given.
Look for His face.

Loosen my grip on the parts of the cart.
Put my hands up to heaven.
Give thanks for His goodness.
Reach out to God's heart.

Live, Love, Laugh, and Ride the Ride!

ABOUT THE AUTHOR

Rebecca Real is a mom, grandma, and Human Resource professional, who loves to explore her faith by writing. She was adopted by a dog and two cats and lives with them in Minnesota.

To see more of this author's work, go to http://faithwriters.com/testimonies2.php.

TINGLES OF REASSURING JOY!
By Sandy Ott

My life, like others', is filled with blessings and struggles, moments of both comfort and perseverance, which affirm the sovereignty of God. Few days pass by where my awareness is not affirmed of how incredibly loving and merciful God is and that He has a plan for my future.

At the age of thirty-six, the doctors discovered a softball-sized brain tumor behind my left eye. A lightning strike at my workplace had sent me to the hospital for a precautionary exam where a CT scan first identified the mass. Two days of scans, tests, and physician consultations resulted in the diagnosis changing from a brain tumor to an arachnoid cyst. Having never had reason to have a brain scan prior to this, it had not been discovered, even though the doctors believe it has been present since birth. At that time, the neurosurgeon advised against intervention unless I began to exhibit symptoms and he wanted a repeat scan in six months to make sure the cyst did not change in size.

One rainy Sunday afternoon, seven years later, I was driving home from church. While waiting at a traffic light, I pondered my to do list of lunch prep, laundry, and household chores. The light changed, I looked both ways, and then started across the intersection. I caught a flash of movement to my left, heard a loud crush of crumpling metal, and everything sped up and then, stopped abruptly. A driver had run the red light striking my car in the driver's door. The impact pushed my vehicle across three lanes onto the opposite side of the four-lane highway. God was watching. There were no oncoming vehicles where both cars involved came to a rest.

Although my vehicle was severely damaged, I did not think that I was injured. Confused, a little addled, I discovered I could not open my door. Someone came and checked on me and said they had called 9-1-1. Both the other driver and I had to be extricated from our vehicles, after which, we were transported to the hospital. Examined in the emergency room, I was sent home with minor bumps and bruises. After a few days, though, I began having neck pain, dizziness, and severe headaches, so I sought treatment. After several weeks of unsuccessful physical therapy, new MRIs of my head and neck revealed damaged vertebrae and a marked growth of the arachnoid cyst.

My neurosurgeon closely studied both scans and was deeply concerned. The cervical vertebrae damage was impinging on my spinal cord and the cyst was pushing my optic nerve. He recommended surgical intervention as soon as possible. Honestly, I cannot remember much of what he said beyond the words "brain surgery." My mind and emotions were reeling. *Brain surgery? Spinal surgery? Really?* I kept repeating the questions in my mind.

The surgeon allowed me a short time to consider my options. I obtained a second opinion, which confirmed the seriousness of the situation. After much prayer and consulting with my family, both surgeries were soon scheduled, the brain surgery first and the neck surgery four weeks later.

During the wait, I spent a lot of time praying, begging God to show me why this was happening. I asked family, church friends, and pretty much anyone to pray on my behalf. When it came time for the brain surgery, although I worried about my family, I felt at peace about the operation; I knew I had to trust God. Relief washed over me when my doctor joined hands with my family in the pre-op area to pray for a successful outcome. As I heard him ask God to guide his hands, it confirmed to me that God was present and, whatever the result, all would be God's Will.

Seven hours later, the doctor came out and spoke with my husband. "She had an actively bleeding subdural hematoma that should have killed her. I can't believe she was able to walk in on her own with that kind of damage." With a huge smile, he proclaimed, "God's not done with her yet."

The routine one-night stay in the ICU turned into a three-day stint as I recovered from the blood loss and a more invasive operation. The neck surgery was completed four weeks later.

During most of my twelve-week-long recovery, I could not focus my eyes well enough to read, but I spent a lot of time praying. After four years, the only long-lasting physical effect I have is a tingling prickly sensation on the left side of my face caused by the facial nerve being severed. However, the resulting emotional and spiritual trials permanently altered my perception of God and perspective on life.

For the last four years, I have experienced that tingling sensation and a tired droopy feeling on the left side of my face, particularly if I am exhausted or stressed. Instead of being discouraged or disheartened by this weakness, this uncomfortable sensation serves as an encouraging reminder of the miracle God produced in my life.

I have replayed the events over in my mind, searching for what I could or should learn from the experience. God allowed me to see Heaven revealed through the support of my family, friends, and the actions of an unashamed Christian neurosurgeon. Words like amazing, awesome, powerful, merciful have been used to describe God, but sometimes it takes recognizing a true miracle to comprehend His power and character. Acknowledging the depth of His love and appreciating the breadth of His plan came only after the roots were planted deep in my heart reaching the very core of my spirit.

Through this intricately orchestrated chain of events, I realized that God indeed is omniscient. He does not make mistakes. I had a benign cyst on my brain since birth; it had never caused me any problems, yet, forty-three years later, God used it to cushion my brain, preventing damage from a massive neurological hemorrhage. The sovereign hand of God thwarted this condition, which should have ended my life. He always had a plan!

With this knowledge forever emblazoned upon my heart, my single-minded purpose each day is to fervently seek Him, believe Him, and pursue ways to serve in His kingdom. All the adjectives describing God do not adequately express the faith-affirming joy that has eternally marked my soul. Every time I experience that prickly tingling sensation in my face, I feel the reassuring warmth of His hand on my life. All I want to do now is share that joy with others.

ABOUT THE AUTHOR

Sandy Ott lives with her husband, Bill, in Kentucky, USA. They have a daughter, Krysten, and a son-in-law, Josh. She enjoys reading, writing, and serving her church and other community organizations. She has worked in the emergency services for over twenty-five years.

To see more of this author's work, go to http://faithwriters.com/testimonies2.php.

DANCING WITH THE DEVIL
By Sheldon Bass

In a cold jail cell, over two decades ago, withdrawals from heroin, cocaine, and various pills detached my tortured mind from reality. Lying on my back in a pool of sweat and vomit, the room spun out of control, just as my life had.

Since age eleven, I'd called myself a Christian. Then, at seventeen, I was introduced to the party lifestyle and began smoking pot. Still attending church, I played the part; I'd never take the Lord's name in vain, refused to steal, or listen to music that sounded evil. When party mates cursed in God's name, I'd be offended and told them so.

Over a decade later, I was facing twenty-five years in prison for parole and probation violations, and a new charge for possession. My body went limp. *My life is over,* I thought.

I wailed out to God, as I'd done many times whenever my lifestyle had gotten me into hot water.

But this time was different: the Lord refused to respond.

He'd always accepted me back before—always forgiven me. But my Savior knew the perfect wake-up call for me; I needed to understand the darkness I'd chosen over Him, and what it is like to be completely void of peace. One terrifying thought blared in my head: *Have I strayed too far?*

Staring at the ceiling, I felt like I was inside a scrap-metal crusher, and realizing my own stupidity added to the pressure bearing down on my soul. Empty inside and hopeless, black despair enveloped my being.

Suddenly, a personification of the devil himself appeared in my cell, accompanied by two demons. I remember thinking how strange their evil laughter sounded, because there was no joy in it. They too were miserable. Satan's horrifying words brought the metal crusher down full force, "You belong to me now. God is finished with you. You're all out of second chances."

Then two of the most gruesome creatures any mind could imagine hovered over my aching body. Their faces were like a depiction of space-aliens, gray and misshapen, with huge, elongated skulls. Slobbery slime oozed from their thin lips and dripped onto my face. Desperately, I tried to wipe it away, but they grabbed hold of my arms, still laughing, as their clammy hands lifted me onto my feet. I found myself looking straight into their cold, empty, lifeless eyes. One demon mockingly held me in his spectral arms and twirled around in a devilish dance, as if to romance me.

I thought I'd known fear before that day. Yet nothing could describe the deep-seated dread I felt. At the apex of fright, I blacked out.

When I awoke, I was in a new cell. Immediately, I crashed to my knees on the unforgiving concrete floor, and cried aloud to Jesus, "Mercy! Lord, have mercy on me!"

During these, the darkest hours of my life, my heart ached with desperation. I'd cut myself off from my well of hope. I needed the peace that goes beyond all physical circumstances; the same peace I'd experienced in my past relationship with the Savior of the world.

In the tiny cell, there was a small steel table welded to the steel wall, which matched the steel bars and bunk. There, lay a newspaper glowing in a halo of light as if it were calling me. I didn't recognize the publication, *The Christian Inmate News*.

The cover announced an article titled 'The Prince of Peace.'

I thought, *I wrote an article with the same title and submitted it to...* I couldn't remember where. Drugs had fried my memory. Scrambling to that column, my own name was listed as the author.

*It **is** my article!*

I'd submitted it over a year prior. As I read, waves of warm comfort washed over me. The tension ebbed from my body, along with the pain.

How ironic is it that the words I'd written nearly two years before that day, during a one-month stint in county jail, would be the exact words I needed to hear just then? Writing of Jesus, I'd said, "Sometimes He lets the storms rage, allowing the wind and waves to go wild, and He instead calms His children, delivering us safely through the storm."

Afterwards, I lifted my head and stretched out my hands toward Heaven. I could sense the powerful and loving embrace of Jesus. My spirit heard those sweet words I so longed to hear,

"You are forgiven."

Again and again, I'd heard those comforting words from my Savior.

How can He forgive me, yet again? What kind of love is so great? Only His! Finally, I surrendered completely to God's will. He has empowered me to live the kind of life that pleases Him, and to never abuse drugs again. Before then, I'd been double-minded, refusing to let go of things I thought brought comfort. But only Jesus has the comfort I need.

Engulfed in peace, my shouts echoed down the corridor, "I'm forgiven!"

The chaplain had no idea how that newspaper ended up in my cell. It was (and still is) his responsibility to approve all such reading material before it entered the prison.

I asked, "Are there any more copies?"

"*Christian Inmate News*? Never heard of it!"

Suddenly, I wasn't so concerned with how long I'd spend in prison. Jesus was with me! In His mercy, God reduced my time behind bars to only two years out of a possible twenty-five. During those twenty-four months, glorious things began to happen.

One day a hulking, muscle-bound guard strode to my cell and extended a bundle of letters, all addressed to me. I said, "But nobody even knows I'm here!"

The letters were responses to my published article from inmates all over the country. They too needed the peace that transcends all understanding. But, as the Lord gave me words to write back to them, a problem presented itself: the law states that inmates cannot send mail to another institution.

Then, how did their letters reach me? I wondered.

I had no one to relay return messages for me, so I mailed my replies anyway. Twelve men had written in response to that article, and I answered all of them. Every single correspondence went through, regardless of the rule of non-communication between institutions. Most of them continued to write back, expressing transformations taking place in their hearts. It was cause for great joy and celebration.

Transferred to where I'd serve my time, I was approached by the chaplain who knew me from worship services. "I need an assistant, you interested?"

I must've been beaming. "Are you kidding? You bet I am!"

The position offered freedom of movement, trust, and a computer to write on. I led services, preached, taught the bible, counselled the men, and gave my testimony countless times. I even wrote a praise song, performing it at a prison seminar for five-hundred men. The Lord was grooming me for the ministry in which I am engaged today.

Completing my education in and out of prison, I became an ordained minister of the Gospel of Christ.

Jesus is a mighty Savior, who can do all things. He salvaged this life from the scrap heap to display His glory. He's given me position, honor, and respect, but most of all, love! My life has proven God's word true. *"...Whatsoever a man soweth, that shall he also reap..." (Galatians 6:7 KJV)*

ABOUT THE AUTHOR

Sheldon K Bass, author of the book *Meet Him on the Mountain*, is a Christian minister with a passion for people of all cultures. Actively engaged as a community leader and speaker, he brings spiritual perspective to several Indianapolis organizations.

To see more of this author's work, go to http://faithwriters.com/testimonies2.php.

THREE CORDS
By Shann Hall-LochmannVanBennekom

Looking at the clock, I saw it was 2:15 in the afternoon, and I sighed. I hadn't accomplished a thing all day. I dragged my weary body out to the kitchen and saw the overwhelming pile of dishes in the sink. *How did I end up on the bathroom floor? Just a minute ago, I was going to tackle the dishes.* Moaning, I looked around and rubbed the back of my head.

I stood and hobbled into my bedroom and looked at the clock again. *I must be seeing it wrong.* I moved closer. The clock indeed showed I had lost nearly two hours. A chill washed over me.

I realized I couldn't put off going to the epilepsy center any longer. Because of my agoraphobia and the fact that Mom had died at the hospital where the testing would be done, it had been almost two years since the neurologist first arranged for me to go, so he could run tests and discover why I was losing time.

Things were uneventful at the hospital. Considering the fact that I'd endured constant chronic pain for over twenty years, I didn't feel too horrible. Friends and family visited me as my head was covered with EEG electrodes for tracing my brain waves. A camera and microphone followed me and recorded everything.

After about ten days, the doctor didn't believe my loss of time episodes were seizure-related. I could go home the next day. I felt frustrated. Once again, the doctors had no answers for me. *Could I be crazy?*

The next day I woke up feeling miserable. My stomach turned every time I moved. Soon I was heaving over a basin. When the doctor came in to see me, I was in mid-vomit. "I can't send you home like this. I'll order some medicine to stop the nausea, and if you're better tomorrow, we can send you home."

That night, I felt uneasy. My ribs hurt from the constant vomiting. At 10 PM, the nurse came in with a sip of water and handed me a cup of pills. I swallowed them gingerly, waited a minute to see if they would stay down, then turned on my side, and drifted off.

I remember dreaming that I was visiting my daughter at her house and collapsed on the bathroom floor. Her husband rushed me to the hospital; I could hear doctors in the room yelling out orders. I had no doubt that I was dying.

Suddenly three cords appeared at my side. As I felt my spirit leave my body, I grabbed the closest cord. It was red and filled me with anger and hate. I immediately dropped it and grabbed the silver cord. Unexpectedly, I saw my three kids and my husband huddled down the hall. The pain seared my body. I felt as though I was being burned alive. I tried to scream, "I don't want to die," but nothing came out.

Out of the corner of my eye, I could see the glow of the gold cord. In my heart, I knew if I grabbed it, I would die. All my life, I've had a horrible death phobia. There have been times when the thought of dying freaked me out so much I actually climbed up the wall, screaming while stepping on the headboard, grabbing pictures to steady myself, hoisting myself up by tugging at the curtain until my feet rested on the windowsill, and the curtain rod and I came crashing down.

Three Cords

The fear became more manageable over time, but never entirely went away. I can't say how many times I prayed that God would give me a life-after-death experience like the ones I had read about in books.

Knowing I was dying while my kids sobbed down the hall was too much. The panic screamed as it ravished my body. I don't think I had ever been so terrified and in so much pain. Finally, I couldn't bear it any longer. I grabbed the gold cord. The pain was still intense, but the panic subsided. I looked around, and when I realized I could no longer see my family, my stomach plunged. I dropped the gold cord and clung to the silver one. Once again, my kids came back into focus. I could hear them crying, and one said, "I don't want Mommy to die."

The panic built up again; I couldn't tolerate it anymore, so again, I dropped the silver cord and clung to the gold one just long enough to allow my body some tiny relief, and then I went back to the silver, so I could see my family again. I had been praying the whole time, but didn't feel comforted.

My minister had dropped in several times earlier in the week. I thought of him, and I called out. "Jamie, where are you? I need a sermon."

I heard a voice clearly respond. "Hold on, Shann, just hold on."

Suddenly, I realized that all my life, I had what I believed was a strong faith in God. I knew I had to trust that Jesus would care for my kids. It wouldn't be easy to lose their mom, but I knew he would take care of them. I grabbed the silver cord one more time and mentally said my goodbyes. Fully accepting the fact that I would die, I grabbed the gold cord with both hands and held on.

The next thing I knew I woke up in the ICU. A nurse called my name. "Do you know where you are?"

I pried my eyes open and blinked. "The hospital." I couldn't remember the name of it or which city it was in or even that I had spent the prior ten days in it. As the nurse and doctor continued to care for me, things slowly came into focus.

"Where's my family?" I felt sick, thinking they must be panic-stricken by now.

"Do you want me to call them? It's two in the morning; they're probably asleep."

"They aren't here?" My mind began to clear some more, and I realized everything I just experienced must have been a dream.

The nurse interrupted my thoughts. "You had us scared. I thought you were a goner."

The next day my minister came in to see me. I looked at him and asked, "Where were you last night when I called your name?"

I told him the story as I watched the color drain from his face and his mouth flop open. "What time was this?"

I shrugged. "Between ten and two."

He looked at me with wide eyes. "I heard someone call my name. I sat up trembling because Momma isn't doing well, and I thought it might have been her. God reassured me that my mom was okay. He told me to pray for the person, and I did. Then, I fell back asleep."

I realized this dream was far more than a dream. God granted me this vision for a purpose—to lessen my fears. Because of what happened, the doctors determined severe sleep apnea was causing a good deal of my health problems. They may have never discovered it if not for my near-death experience. My phobias are slowly lessening with time, and I feel better than I have in twenty-five years. I never dreamed I'd thank God for puke, but I believe that it saved my life, so I am grateful.

ABOUT THE AUTHOR

Shann Hall-LochmannVanBennekom and her husband Christopher live in western New York. They have three wonderful children, Emily, Quinten, and Lydia. Shann is looking forward to becoming a grandmother in May when Emily and her husband Andy deliver their first child.

To see more of this author's work, go to http://faithwriters.com/testimonies2.php.

ASK AND YOU WILL RECEIVE
By Graham Keet

The mobile phone vibrated urgently in my shirt pocket. Not wanting to disturb the meeting, I left the boardroom quietly and answered the call from a number I did not recognize.

"Is that Mr. Graham Keet?" a female voice asked.

"Yes."

"Father of Gary Keet?"

"Yes." Distant alarm bells rang.

"Mr. Keet, this is Linda Rothman from Sterling Airborne Surveys in Johannesburg. I regret to advise you that your son Gary was killed at ten o'clock this morning when their aircraft crashed shortly after takeoff from Nampula airport in Mozambique. We have confirmed that both Gary and the pilot were killed on impact."

Silence.

"Mr. Keet, are you there?"

"Yes, I'm here. Are you sure about this?" I was too stunned to offer anything remotely resembling a sensible response. "Is there not some mistake?"

There was no mistake. That morning of the 20th April 2004 marked the beginning of a new spiritual roller-coaster journey for my wife Astrid and me. The turmoil that invades a parent's mind at a time like this is unimaginable, and nothing can prepare one for the agony that follows.

I clearly remembered praying for Gary early that morning, asking the Lord to keep him safe in the air, during takeoff and landing. *Did God not hear my prayers? Perhaps I did not deserve to have them answered? If this is the case, then what more should I have done?* Astrid and I had both been Sunday school teachers in the past and were currently hosting a weekly young-adults group in our home. Had we missed something, or was it all just a waste of time? *Is God not really concerned about us?* Questions and yet more questions, but no answers that made any sense.

As Christian parents, our first concern was whether Gary was now in Heaven with the Lord. He was thirty-one years old and was unmarried. He had qualified at university as a construction manager, but had left the construction industry to pursue his first love: flying. He had started private flying lessons with a friend of his, who is a qualified instructor, and Gary had secured a job with an airborne survey company as an operator of surveying equipment until he qualified as a pilot.

Our concern stemmed from the fact that Gary had a very restless spirit; he never really seemed to be at peace with his circumstances or within himself. He had lived on both sides of the fence. He was active in our church and a cameraman on the media team, yet he had a group of friends, who enjoyed night clubbing on a regular basis.

Gary was an extrovert, who lived life to its fullest and enjoyed pastimes like bungee jumping, skydiving, and driving fast cars. Gary was a leader among his friends, which gave us confidence that he would not exceed the limits provided by his upbringing. But how could we be sure?

Then the Lord started to work His miracles. In the morning, about three days after the accident, Astrid woke me, her face glowing with excitement. "God has answered our prayers," she said, her face radiant. "Gary is in Heaven with Jesus."

"But how do you know?" I was not yet fully awake, but could sense Astrid's excitement.

"Have you ever read 1 Samuel 14?" she asked, and without waiting for an answer, she opened her Bible and started reading the account of a battle between the Israelites and the Philistines. "The important part," she said excitedly, "is that some of the Hebrews had gone over to the Philistines, but when God shook the earth and caused confusion in the Philistine ranks, many of those Hebrews went back to the Israelite camp. God has assured me that Gary was in His camp when he died."

She had tears in her eyes now. "God wants us to know that what He has done may seem cruel in our eyes, but He knows the bigger picture, and He has taken Gary at exactly the right time."

After reading 1 Samuel 14 myself and admitting I had never seen this particular passage of Scripture, I too realized that God was speaking to us through His Word.

In the days that followed, the Lord provided further confirmation. We received Gary's bag of personal belongings, sent by his company from Mozambique. With heavy hearts, we opened the bag and unpacked it. Our heaviness turned to joy when we saw that the books he had taken with him were two of John Maxwell's books on Christian leadership and Bruce Wilkinson's *The Dream Giver*. With tears in my eyes, I opened *The Dream Giver* and read how a Nobody named Ordinary could realize his Big Dream. Flying had been Gary's big dream.

We received further confirmation when Hendrik, Gary's flying instructor and a born-again Christian, visited us and told us that the day before the accident Gary had telephoned him from Mozambique to say that his dream of flying was being realized and that he was at last feeling contented with his life. He told Hendrik that he had just finished reading *The Dream Giver* and was at peace with himself and his world.

In the weeks that followed, many of his friends visited our home, most of them relating the positive influence Gary had been in their lives. We even learned that some of the girls in his circle of friends would not date a boy unless Gary had met the guy and given his okay. Such was the esteem in which his judgment was held.

Then finally, we found the transcription of a prophecy that had been spoken over Gary a few years earlier, which confirmed everything the Lord had revealed to us up to that time. It read:

> My son, you have looked over the fence and seen all the things that are happening in the world, many times desired to join there and to follow the excitement that is happening on the other side, but I have kept you firmly rooted on the good side of the wall.
>
> Now I want you to redirect those prayers outside, over the fence to those people you have looked at, and to those people you have seen wandering in the darkness, who are wandering with nowhere to go and nobody to follow. You will know me, says God. Man-to-man you will know me; deep calling unto deep, says God, for I will visit you.

"That explains why Gary had such a diverse circle of friends," I said to Astrid. "How else could those people be reached?"

The death of a child can place an enormous strain on a marriage, but in our case, it bonded us together in God's love. We know now that He is never far from any of His children, and we have the certainty that "...*in all things God works for the good of those who love him, who have been called according to his purpose.*" *(Rom 8: 28 NIV)*

[Note: Fictitious names are used for the airborne company and its personnel.]

ABOUT THE AUTHOR

Graham Keet is a retired telecom engineer living in Pretoria, South Africa with his wife Astrid. He plays guitar and currently leads worship in their weekly home group. His other hobbies are reading, training in the gym, and archery.

To see more of this author's work, go to http://faithwriters.com/testimonies2.php.

LIVING THE FAITH
By Edmond Ng

While I was still in high school, I did something that upset my parents so greatly that they had me starved, disciplined, and locked up on occasions. I received Jesus as my Lord and Savior, an act my parents deemed as rebellious and a violation of trust. Throughout the genealogy of my family, every member has been a follower of a hybrid Buddhism and Taoism religion. In my parents' eyes, what I did was unforgivable, and for many years since, I was persecuted.

Initially, my parents tried to bring me back into their fold by punishing me. Eventually, they gave me up as lost after I repeatedly refused to participate in their religious practices, which included ancestral worship and bowing down to idols. I became to my parents as one who had gone astray and did not know my own roots, and to the people of the community, a renegade and an outcast. In school, I was ridiculed and nicknamed "holy cow," and was segregated from a circle of friends. Several years passed before the people I knew gradually accepted me for who I am. Nevertheless, even until this day, I face rejections and displeasure at times from members of my family and relatives, especially during occasions such as non-Christian funerals because of my refusal to participate in the rites.

All these sufferings, however, are insignificant in comparison to the sufferings the Lord went through for me.

Whatever I had gained in the past, I now count it all lost for the sake of Christ because of the surpassing value of knowing Him as my Lord and Savior (Philippians 3:7-8). What a joy to trust in Jesus! When things seem hopeless, and even at times when I stray, God has never once turned me away. He is always present and near to fill my heart with calm that surpasses understanding and empowers me to continue with confidence.

After more than thirty years in the faith, I have been privileged to serve the Lord in many areas, including church youth ministry and cell group leadership, worship leading, gospel events counseling, and new converts nurturing. I have also been privileged to write Christian articles for church newsletters and Christian magazines.

Today, I am serving the Lord and ministering to His people through devotional writing at various online Christian communities, and my heart's desire is to share with everyone the inner peace I have in Jesus.

ABOUT THE AUTHOR

Edmond Ng is a freelance writer for print and digital media who writes online for various Christian communities. He has served in many areas of Christian ministry and completed a course with a Bible seminary under a continuing education program for lay leadership training.

To see more of this author's work, go to http://faithwriters.com/testimonies2.php

EMPTY
By Rachel Malcolm

I collapsed to my knees and rocked back and forth in agony. My arms hugged my abdomen protectively as I wept and mouthed my silent prayer. *Oh, God! Please don't take this baby from me. I can't endure this. You know how I love this precious gift. Our children prayed for this baby.*

The next couple of hours would bring a storm of physical agony and soul anguish that I was wholly unprepared to weather and then leave me empty—so very empty. That night I lay curled in a ball, my husband sleeping, the children sleeping. My tears were all spent and I lay exhausted, but sleep evaded me. *Why, God? Why?*

I had known that one out of every eight pregnancies ends in miscarriage, but I had never let my mind dwell on the possibility. *I just wouldn't be able to deal with it,* I told myself. But here I was, and what a lonely journey I found it to be.

"This is why expecting mothers didn't use to tell people about their pregnancies until they were past twelve weeks," a friend gently admonished me when I told her it was hard to tell others about the miscarriage. *Are we supposed to just suffer alone, then?* I got the message: good people don't talk about miscarriages. We are not supposed to grieve the loss of the unborn, or if we do, it must be done quietly. A miscarriage is dark—somehow dirty. And so we struggle along in isolation, because of some obscure veil of superstition.

At only ten weeks gestation, a graveyard burial wasn't an option. Instead, we chose a spot on a hill overlooking a quiet and remote lake. I laid a piece of paper in the grave with the name ***Jonathan*** written in blue crayon. It was the only thing I could give my baby—a name.

I lingered at the grave after my husband and children had gone back to the van and fingered the rocks my children had placed on the grave. Some were round and smooth, and one was pinkish and almost heart-shaped. I breathed in the woody scent of evergreen trees, moist earth, and damp moss and let my tears flow. I finally stood to leave, but my steps were heavy. I turned back once to look at the little sun-streaked grave on the hill.

The next two weeks were strange as I tried to reconcile grief with living. The first time I laughed, it felt unnatural—almost wrong. Normalcy was returning, but just under the surface was a hole of anguish that could re-open at any time.

It seemed like there were babies and pregnant women everywhere, and just the sight of one or the other could bring on a flood of tears in the grocery store or bank. I unknowingly covered my heart with a shield of anger to protect myself from the relentless grief.

Sitting in the doctor's waiting room, I noticed a pregnant woman walk across the room and sit across from me. My heart began to race and my hands clenched into fists. Dark bitterness washed over me. *Oh God, I used to experience such joy at seeing a baby or a pregnant woman and now I feel anger, jealousy, and bitterness.* Tears stung my eyes as I begged God to restore my joy.

At church, comments meant to comfort only brought more despair. *Please help me, God,* I silently prayed as I tried in vain to worship. I placed my hands over my mouth as the song "Blessed Be Your Name" by Matt and Beth Redman began. Every word pierced me. Tears coursed down my cheeks as I felt God calling me to praise Him for His goodness—even when He takes away. My throat tight with emotion, I silently sang the words with my entire being.

That moment of surrender was the beginning of the thaw in my heart. God's love wrapped around me like light, and He brought me into a deeper, more restful, relationship with Him. I was changed by the loss, but not for the worse. I was becoming more sensitive to others—more aware of the pain others were experiencing. God had placed a desire in my heart to reach out to other women who had experienced the loss of their little ones due to miscarriage, abortion, stillbirth, or infant death.

One morning, as I walked outside, I saw a vivid image in my mind of a little blond boy with blue eyes. I knew that he was my Jonathan. Love coursed through me. "Mommy!" he said as he ran into my open arms. I just sat down on the gravel and wept.

Pain and joy were so intermingled that I couldn't distinguish between the two. Before seeing this nearly tangible image, there had only been hurt. The vision brought a beautiful truth to my heart: I have a child in Heaven. I never had the opportunity to rock him to sleep or tickle his tiny toes, but one day I will hold him. And nothing can take away that joy.

ABOUT THE AUTHOR

Rachel Malcolm lives in northern, British Columbia, Canada, with her husband and six rambunctious children. She spends her spare time curled up with a book or tapping out stories on her laptop with some chocolate and a cup of weak tea nearby.

To see more of this author's work, go to http://faithwriters.com/testimonies2.php

A LESSON LEARNED FROM MY DEAD UNCLE
By Clyde Blakely

My uncle died before I was born. In fact, he died before *he* was born. He was Granddad's first child and only son, but I never knew if he was named. Granddad never talked about it; Grandma did only once, in passing. I believe the tragedy of my uncle being stillborn was part of God's plan. Did Granddad and Grandma comprehend right away the good God had in mind, or did they see it later? Salty tears often obscure our spiritual vision.

Ninety years ago, Granddad was a drunk and a rabble-rouser. Haunted by his son's stillbirth, life-and-death issues, and the whys of life's tragedies, Granddad searched for answers. It turned out he only needed one. He found that Jesus was the answer to all life's questions, and the Lord Jesus turned Granddad's loss to gain.

He took Jesus as his Lord and Savior and entered the ministry. In the next four generations, a majority of his descendants and an untold number in his circuit-riding church congregations accepted the Lord. I sat under Granddad's teaching, and while a senior in high school, I accepted Jesus as my Savior. For both of us, it was a reward. Shortly before he died, Granddad baptized me, and I remember praising God with Granddad when I came up out of the water.

A Lesson Learned from My Dead Uncle

I never really considered what influence my uncle's death had on Granddad until I experienced life's untoward events. As a Critical Care and Emergency Room RN, I participated in about 1,000 resuscitations—some successful and some unsuccessful. With each event came a family for me to rejoice with or to comfort.

I was able to relate to these families because I'd lived through my own hard experiences, and especially ones that brought me closer to Jesus and helped me grow in the Lord. I was born with a heart defect, and I experienced an unrelated heart infection. I nearly drowned and came close to bleeding to death three times. Two sisters have died. Both my parents are in Heaven.

While I served as mayor of a small community, I endured unjustified and devastating character attacks, and my family moved out of town. The day after Christmas, when we'd been in our new home only eleven days, an electrical short sparked a fire that destroyed the house and all our things. We barely escaped with what we wore; two of us had burns that required medical attention. Watching the fire consume our worldly possessions, God started to create in me a better opinion of my fellow man and to show me that the most important possessions here on earth are Jesus, family, and friends.

Over the next several months, I was a witness to the love of God, sharing with many, some of whom had also lost their homes. Through the love of the community showered on my family, the Lord strengthened my trust in Him, literally by faith through fire.

When I "accidentally" (speaking in human terms) suffered a shotgun accident, not knowing if I'd live or die, I stood alone holding my spurting carotid artery. I knew this situation was from God. I didn't blame Him, only searched for what He had planned for me. I knew if I died, I'd be in His presence in perfect love, peace, and forgiveness with no time for confessions or change of lifestyle. There was no fear in that knowledge. Perhaps one could call this faith under gunfire.

After I recovered, I carried around a picture of the x-ray showing the pellets in my chest, neck, and face. When greeted with "How are you?" (which was quite often) I replied, "I feel shot," and then I pulled out the x-ray film.

Immediately my little audience was engrossed in the x-ray, and I gave a short version of what had happened, followed by a testimony of God's love. One day I witnessed to nine people in forty-five minutes! How often is someone given that privilege?

One day I asked my pastor, "When can God start to take the bad things that happen to us and turn them into good for a witness of Him, as the Bible says?" I had already recognized the answer: As soon as we turn the bad thing over to Him.

When Granddad gave to God the stillborn death of his son, it was only then God was able to start using it for good. It worked the same for me after the house fire and being shot. At first, I was surprised the Lord Jesus stayed with me through all this trouble, and by relying on Him, I was not only comforted, I actually grew. The Lord was always there, whether I could see Him or not.

For some life events, I still haven't seen His divine plan, but since He has my good in mind (Jeremiah 29:11), I've learned to rely on Him during those periods of silence. He has granted me a peace the world can't give. I pray that whatever the outcome, Jesus will be glorified.

A year ago, I was diagnosed with cancer, and at first, I felt numb. But the Lord has already gently lifted me and shown me His loving grace. His plan is to make me more like Him. I also know that when I see Jesus face to face all my tears will be wiped away, plus—when I meet him—I will learn my uncle's name.

Almost 100 years have passed since my uncle's birth/death, and it is easier now to see beyond the tragedy to praise

God for His working. Such is the privilege of hindsight. Struggling to better understand my times of trouble, even with the periods of God's sometimes confusing silence, has drawn me closer to Him, for I know He sees the future more clearly than we see the past.

In an Instant

Sudden, the sirens, quick prayer?
It is time to meet the Maker
In an Instant

No time for reflection
No time for confession

Winging heavenward
Eternal joy as the reward

In an Instant
Oh Glory divine

In that Instant
To see His beautiful face

In that Instant
Saved by His wondrous grace

Clyde Blakely
30 May 08

"'For I know the plans I have for you,' declares the LORD, 'plans to prosper you and not to harm you, plans to give you hope and a future.'" (Jeremiah 29:11 NIV)

ABOUT THE AUTHOR

Clyde Blakely is a semi-retired RN, who loves to write on Christian topics. He lives with his wife on a small farm in his native Oregon.

To see more of this author's work, go to http://faithwriters.com/testimonies2.php

MY TESTIMONY
By Frances Seymour

When I was six years old, I contracted rheumatic fever—an infection that can affect the heart. While in the hospital, a blood clot formed in my heart, moved to my brain and burst, paralyzing me on the left side. My future looked dim.

Fortunately, we had one heart specialist in Charlotte, North Carolina, and Dr. Robicheck quickly performed an experimental procedure to remove the fluid from around my heart. The experiment was successful. The paralysis left. But, the doctors warned, "When she goes back to school, she could be slow to learn; perhaps even slightly mentally retarded. We don't know what kind of damage the blood clot has caused."

Amazingly, my school grades never faltered (unless, of course, I allowed them to). I graduated from high school while I was still seventeen years old. Later on, I took some college courses and held a highly visible job in planning and inventory control for many years. On the surface, all seemed well. But, I was carrying around a deep, heavy secret.

Let me pause here and share with you that I really gave my heart to Jesus when I was fifteen years old. However, the truth is I did not surrender my life to His lordship until I was in my thirties. What a difference that choice made! All young people should understand this truth. If you've given your heart to Jesus, but you're continuing to live life your way, let go and let God! He's much more capable of running things than you are. Believe me.

Now, here's my secret. You see, the day after I graduated from high school, I experienced my first black-out spell, as I called them. My mom called them blank stares. My little sister grew to call them "those things."

As I was coming around one day, I overheard her say to my niece, "Oh she's just having one of those things; she'll be okay in a minute."

Regardless of what we called my affliction, the truth was I was stricken with a mild form of epilepsy. I was so ashamed. You see, I grew up in the '70s when there were a lot of misconceptions about epilepsy and even a stigma attached to this misunderstood illness. I went to school with a girl, who suffered from severe seizures. Other children laughed and poked fun at her. Then they said hurtful things behind her back. She was so sweet, and I easily befriended her.

I'm sure the shame I felt came from recalling how painful it was for my friend all through school. I simply did not want to go through that. Fortunately, my seizures mostly began after I was out of school. They usually occurred when I was extremely tired or as I was drifting off to sleep. You might say that I lived many years in a closet. I was afraid that someone important was going to find out about my well-kept secret, especially an employer. I cannot tell you how many times I cried, prayed, and petitioned God to get rid of the seizures for me, to heal me if that was His will. Somehow, I knew deep down in my heart that it could happen.

Then in the early fall of 1998, an absolute godsend stepped into my life. His name was Dr. Steven Karner. After a few visits with this doctor and a couple medicine changes, Dr. Karner sat me down and said, "Frances, after reviewing your case history and where I believe the focal point of your seizures to be, I think you are a prime candidate for brain surgery."

He was excited. Let me assure you that I did not share his enthusiasm. I think it's probably safe to say that I was scared. Dr. Karner went on to say, "This won't happen overnight. Preparation for the surgery will take several months. You'll be in and out of the hospital. There will be a series of mental, physical, and psychological tests."

He was right; all that had to be done. Finally, the surgery date arrived. On June 19, 1999, a group of highly skilled neurosurgeons at Carolina's Medical Center went to work and performed a right temporal lobectomy—the removal of a portion of my right temporal lobe. Today, I am more than fifteen-years seizure-free and completely off seizure medications. Enthusiastically, I give God all the praise, honor, and glory.

I realize that many things could've happened. I could've been paralyzed for the rest of my life or mentally challenged. The worst-case scenario is that I could've died. Yet God has allowed me to be here to tell you that miracles do still happen. I'm walking proof. Prayer changes things.

Sometimes it may take months or even years to come by, but keep holding on. Keep on praying, and don't give up. And lastly, but even more importantly, can I tell you that God wants your heart, too?

That's right! Not the small portion that you may be willing to offer up right now. Oh no, God wants and deserves so much more than that. He wants your whole heart. All of it!

"For I know the plans I have for you, declares the Lord. They are plans to prosper you, not to harm you. They are plans to give you a future and a hope." (Jeremiah 29:11 NIV)

ABOUT THE AUTHOR

Frances Seymour is the author of three Christian books: *The Significance of a Dream, An Inspirational Book of Poetry and Short Stories, Perils and Promises, Life on Mission,* and *Mediocrity to Maturity, A Journey from Despair to Repair.* She lives in Monroe, North Carolina, USA.

To see more of this author's work, go to http://faithwriters.com/testimonies2.php.

FAITH IN THE FOG
By Carla Rogers

Watching the rain streak down the passenger window, I realized my soul was just as cold. The wipers and rain blared compared to the quiet hush in the car. I shivered at the thought of my lost friendships, betrayals, and just plain loss over the past few years. As my husband concentrated on driving, I quietly sobbed, though I didn't want him to hear. I was ashamed of doubting God's love for me and of my overwhelming fear that God was not trustworthy. I knew I was disappointing God at every turn.

"Do you ever wonder why testing happens?" I asked my husband. "How can a God who is good allow such pain, such heartache? I know that he is in control, why isn't he helping?"

"I have the same questions," he said. "But you can never lose faith."

It was easy for him to say. I had said the same thing many times to others in their times of trial. But now this was my trial, not theirs. I knew that despair should never be in a Christian's life, but that only made it worse. Despair comes when God hides, and my soul was dying a slow death.

Many, many verses in the Bible talk about God hiding or turning his face. I never really understood those verses until this trial. David wrote, *"Do not hide Your face from me; Do not turn Your servant away in anger; You have been my help;*

*Do not leave me nor forsake me, O God of my salvation."
(Psalm 27:9 NASB)*

These phrases also turn up in Job. I was slowly beginning to realize that God hiding isn't a new concept.

Remarkably, even though I had read the Bible many times through the years and always found hope, it seemed like nothing I read relieved my hopelessness. I didn't believe anymore that God was good, or at least he didn't love me anymore. I slowly stopped studying God's Word and stopped praying because I felt like God had stopped communicating to me. The feeling that I couldn't gain God's acceptance, that I was always a disappointment caused me to pull away.

The nightmare had started innocently enough. Several friends betrayed me. I have been betrayed by close friends before, but this time was different. Spiritual attacks always strike at the foundations of one's soul. I lost most of my friendships because I didn't know whom to trust. Since I didn't want to be a gossip or a murderer of someone's ministry, I didn't confide in anyone, and I fell prey to one of Satan's best tools—isolation.

I couldn't find a way to forgive, no matter how hard I wanted to. Holding onto grudges is Satan's best gateway sin. I didn't really want to forgive. Forgiving is admitting what the other person did was okay, right? Bitterness soon followed, along with doubt, hopelessness, anger, and jealousy—too many sins to count. I had always been taught to never give place to the devil (Ephesians 4:27). At the time, I didn't realize that my bitterness was an open invitation for oppression and bondage; I had given place to the devil.

The Pharisees, even while they were in bondage to Rome, said to Jesus, *"We are Abraham's descendants and have never yet been enslaved to anyone...." (John 8:33a NIV)* That was me. How could I, a Christian since my teenage years, have a problem with bondage and not realize it, but I did.

Friends started asking me what I had done for God to allow this trial. They also told me that I had some hidden sin that God wanted me to repent. If they only knew, but this assumption was not correct. But because of that line of thinking, I began to think that I had to do something to get back into God's good graces. Along with all the other sins that I had begun to accumulate, the sin of *good works* started. I just knew if I had the right Biblical revelation, the right good works, or got rid of generational curses that God would bless me again. All this led to was feeling like I was disappointing God even more. It took a while to realize I was on the wrong path back to God.

I ordered a book on how to listen to God, which was God sent. It taught me how to listen to God even through the fog of oppression. Tentatively, I started my exercises.

"God, many times in your word (Psalm 139:17-18 for one) you state that you think of me often. Would you please reveal to me some of your thoughts of me?"

"Good and faithful servant" came through like a foghorn leading me home. I know this is a well-known Bible verse, but it felt like a warm hug. Could it be that God still loved me?

"God, what do you think about my relationship with you?"

"Well done!"

Tears flowed freely as I felt God's presence for the first time in years. I realized that even with all the sins, false good works, bitterness, and resentment, God still loved me. Our relationship was still in good shape. He started healing me even while I was still harboring bitterness.

He revealed to me past hurts from my childhood and hurts that were more recent–all needed to be healed, including the current betrayal. God revealed, in time, that my motive to forgive was wrong. I wanted to forgive because I expected God to exact revenge. But what if God decided to exact mercy? God had shown me so much mercy during this trial that I had to show mercy to everyone. That didn't mean that their action was okay or that I had to be friends with the people who'd inflicted the hurt. But I did need to allow God to handle the situation anyway he saw fit. With my healing, came forgiveness. It didn't come overnight or easily, but it came.

God also revealed that I don't disappoint him. There is no verse in the Bible concerning what happens when we disappoint God. The only verse that even mentions *disappoint* is, *"Now hope does not disappoint, because the love of God has been poured out in our hearts by the Holy Spirit who was given to us" (Romans 5:5 NASB)*. God was concerned about us believing that God disappoints us.

Later, I wondered how God could forgive me for not even recognizing his voice at times. In the quietness of that moment, I heard his still small voice.

"You are worth—my Son."

That one sentence released in me true freedom from years of oppression. Hallelujah!

ABOUT THE AUTHOR

Carla Rogers is trying to live the Apelles way, tested and approved of Christ. After being married to Mr. Rogers for over twenty years, they have decided to adopt. She loves to unpack Scripture, tell everyone what she's learned, and be a South Carolina girl. To see more of this author's work, go to http://faithwriters.com/testimonies2.php.

WHAT WAS I THINKING?
By LaVonne Wood

This could be the most exciting day of my life, I thought. It was my senior year in college, and I felt strongly that I would win the ladies' position. I could hardly wait. *For once in my life, maybe, I'd be recognized.*

That day, the whole student body would cast their vote for not only the most popular, but also the person who was most caring and loving—the one who best displayed Christian values. They didn't call the winners King and Queen at this Christian college, but in my mind, it was very similar.

Three of us girls were nominated for the position, and I knew the other two girls well. One was very shy, yet had a soft, sweet spirit, enhanced by a deep love for the things of God. The other, in contrast, was very pretty, outspoken, and popular with the guys. Yet I knew just how troubled and insecure she really was. I had prayed with her many times over the past four years.

As I waited for the results, I found my mind wandering back over the events of the years I'd spent in college. I'd arrived at Trinity Bible College in the middle of the school year. Nearly ten years older than most other students, I wondered how I'd fit in. I recently accepted Christ as my Savior and decided I wanted to serve in some kind of ministry, probably as a Christian counselor. When I first started my studies,

I had only one thing on my mind, to get to know God better and serve Him with my whole heart.

Although learning came hard for me, I spent long hours studying and managed to get good grades in most of my classes. I grew spiritually as well, so I thought. I spent hours praying and seeking God. I never missed a church service or the daily chapel services at the school.

Within a year, I held the position of RA (resident assistant) on the first floor of the freshman dorm. By my third year, I was appointed Assistant Dorm Counselor. This position gave me many opportunities to talk and pray with all girls in my dorm. I spent my prayer time thinking of each room on every floor and praying for the occupants in that room. I continued to pray until I had prayed for every girl in the dorm.

As I prayed, my love for the girls grew deeper and stronger. When they came to me for advice, it seemed the Lord would give me just the right words to say. When prayers were answered, I cried and rejoiced with the girls.

In my mind, I developed a firm relationship with every girl who passed through the freshmen dorm those four years. That is how I knew I would certainly get the most votes on election day.

My mind, however, was not prepared for what happened next. The three of us were all on stage awaiting the final count and the announcement of the winners. My heart kept beating faster and faster with excitement and anticipation. Then the moment came when the announcer said, "And this year's winner is..."

My heart sank. It was not *my* name. Instantly I felt tears well up inside. Using everything I had to hold them back, I tried not to show my disappointment. How hard it was to keep smiling as they took the final pictures. I thought it would never end, and I longed to get back to my room, where I could just let the tears flow.

Thoughts kept rushing through my mind. *How could I be so stupid to think they would vote for me? What possessed me to think that God would bless me in such a way? Why would I think that I could compete with younger and more beautiful girls?*

I couldn't seem to shake the depression and feelings of loss. The tears wouldn't stop flowing. I felt so foolish, and I avoided leaving my room the next few days. I thought I should be strong enough in my Christian walk not to let it bother me like this. I didn't want anyone to see me feeling so hurt. How could I go on? I didn't want to face the world and especially other Christians. I felt embarrassed about the way I was reacting to such a little thing.

"Why did you let this happen to me, Lord? Why didn't you answer my prayer? Didn't you see all that I did for those girls, all the time I spent counseling them and praying for them? Is this how you reward those who do your work, Lord?"

Then the Lord spoke to me softly, but clearly. He asked if I remembered a prayer I had prayed when I first started as an RA in the dorm. He reminded me that I had prayed that His name would be glorified and that when the girls received an answer to any prayer I had prayed for them that they would know it came from God.

Of course! What was I thinking? Any help they received and prayers that were answered, it was God they attributed it to, *not me*. I was just the instrument that led them to One who knew the answers. I had no right to try to take the glory for something God had done. It was He who gave me the right things to say as I counseled. He showed me how to pray. It was always Him, not me!

Suddenly I felt the joy come back into my life. God *had* answered my prayer. The girls had given Him praise and honor, as they should. I asked His forgiveness for trying to receive the glory for myself.

Today, I am reminded to always give the glory to God for all answered prayer and to know that my reward comes from Him alone, not from people. What was I thinking?

ABOUT THE AUTHOR

LaVonne Wood lives with her husband Bob in Highmore, South Dakota, USA. She has worked as a pre-school teacher, secretary, mechanic, bakery supervisor, and consignment-store owner. Now, as a writer, her hope is that her life experiences will touch lives and glorify God.

To see more of this author's work, go to http://faithwriters.com/testimonies2.php.

FACING DANGER, FINDING DELIVERANCE
By Trudy Newell

Tehran, Iran
Sunday, February 11, 1979

As the bullets flew, our apartment building shook. My stomach churned, and I trembled. Where was the safest place?

In our third-story apartment Joel, Sara, and I slammed the five doors to the dining room, the central room of the apartment where there were no windows. We shoved the table and chairs aside, and Sara and I plopped pillows around the floor, more comfortable than the wooden chairs. There, the three of us hunkered down to outwait the shooting in the streets.

As a single missionary woman in Iran for seven years, I loved the Persian people. I also felt a real bond with my fellow missionaries and housemates, Joel and Sara. Earlier, before the shooting had started, we'd watched from the balcony of our third-story apartment as hundreds of young men from the newly-formed Revolutionary Militia poured into the main Iranian army base about a hundred feet away. Then the gunfire started and didn't stop for six hours.

As we sat on the pillows in the windowless room, we wondered what the future held, and we joked and laughed with each other. I crocheted three shawls. As I focused on the Lord, the verses I had memorized from the time I was a child floated through my mind and brought me peace. *"Trust in the Lord with all your heart..." (Proverbs 3:5a NIV)* The kettle sang on top of the *bohari* (heater). We drank tea and munched on peanut butter and crackers. Every time the gunfire slowed down, we dashed into the kitchen to refill the kettle and replenish supplies.

Just after 3 PM, the gunfire ceased. Every window in our apartment had been shot out. After five minutes, we stepped out onto the balcony. The Militia was leaving the army camp loaded with booty. Most of the young men were under eighteen. They had stuffed brown blankets with military supplies. With the blankets and guns slung over their shoulders, they looked like hobos, only more menacing, and we laughed.

We discussed what to do. A minor miracle—even in the devastated infrastructure—the phones worked okay. Joel called Bill Jackson, who worked for Bell Helicopter and lived close to the airport. He felt confident that Bell Helicopter would fly me out with his family, and Bill offered to have his driver come pick me up. The driver told me to sit in front with him, which was improper, but safer.

Then began our wild drive through Tehran, dodging the hot spots. Every time we came to a main intersection, the driver shouted, "Duck."

And I did. In my mind ran, *"So do not fear, for I am with you; do not be dismayed, for I am your God" (Isaiah 41:10a NIV).* It was a real comfort. Buildings were gutted and small piles of debris were burning. We took side roads to the Jackson's house, where I helped Bill's wife Joy with kitchen duties while she packed for herself, Bill, and their three children.

Facing Danger, Finding Deliverance

Monday, February 12, 1979

The plan was to spend a night or two at the Hilton Hotel until our flight was ready to leave, so Bill had gone to the Hilton to make arrangements.

About 10 AM Bill called to check on us. After he hung up, on television we heard that employees of Bell Helicopter at the Hilton had been taken hostage. Was it a rumor? We had just spoken with Bill. Just then, pictures of the Militia storming the Hilton filled the TV screen. Joy's face turned white. She sat on the couch with her head between her hands, despair written on her face. She couldn't talk. The kids were crying. I tried to calm everyone—without success.

God was gracious. At 5 PM, Bill walked through the door. He smiled as he told us Bell Helicopter would call to let us know when to check into the Hilton.

Friday, February 16, 1979

Bill got the phone call in the morning, and his landlord suddenly showed up. Bill did not know Farsi, and his landlord did not speak English, but they had more than communication problems. He glared at Bill. Why had he given the household items away? He was the property owner and was entitled to the furniture left behind and all the American goodies! I was diplomatic as I translated, but the landlord left in a huff.

At 2 PM, the five Jacksons and I loaded up and head off to the Hilton and our final farewell to Iran. As Bill carried out the first suitcase, he had a strange expression on his face. The van had four flat tires, compliments of the landlord. Bill shrugged and loaded the suitcases.

We drove to the Hilton on four flat tires, arrived, and unloaded. Bill handed the keys to the doorman and said, "*Befarmod.*" ("Help yourself.") The man's face brightened, and he grinned broadly.

We found our rooms and discovered the Militia had shot out the locks on the doors a few days before. The folks at the Hilton gave us the VIP treatment and a steak dinner. Back in the room with the two girls after supper, I realized the danger we were in.

I asked seven-year-old Becky, "What will you do if you hear gunfire nearby."

"Sit up in bed, and see what's going on," she said.

"You roll off the bed and lie flat on the floor." I didn't tell her to put a pillow over her head, but I wanted her to be prepared.

We got word to be down in the lobby at 4 AM. The instructions were one suitcase per person and a carry-on. We might only be able to take the carry-on with us, have it packed with the absolute necessities. When I prepared the one suitcase I would take, I chose the smaller one because there were indications we'd have to carry our luggage for some distance.

About that time, the maid walked in. She saw the bigger suitcase I was leaving behind, and her face lit up with joy. Seeing her joy as she struggled with the bigger suitcase made the loss easy for me. I drifted off to sleep remembering the verse: *"In peace I will lie down and sleep, for you alone, Lord, make me dwell in safety." (Psalm 4:8 NIV)*

By 3:30 AM, we were down in the lobby. It was empty except for those leaving Iran. Holding their children close, people stood in small groups and talked in low voices. Most of these folks had worked together at Bell. Time passed, and people started getting agitated. At 6:30 AM, the Revolutionary Militia finally showed up, checked passports, and questioned us individually. At 8:30, they loaded us into buses and sent our luggage in trucks behind us.

On our bus, the militia, which consisted of nine young teen boys, toted machine guns. They loaded and unloaded them, playing around. I would have felt safer if they had pointed the guns directly at me!

As we passed the Shahyad monument, tears came to my eyes. I loved my adopted country. My heart bled for the Persian people, and it was hard to leave.

God continued to intervene and to provide for me through the years. I'm thankful for God's protection, and I'm thankful for the privilege of seeing God work in a very dangerous situation.

ABOUT THE AUTHOR

Trudy Newell lives with her husband, Mike, in Georgia and works among Hindus moving into the area. Trudy has served the Lord in Iran, Kenya, Christar headquarters, and England, where she has ministered to both Muslims and Hindus. Trudy writes for *Tween Girls and God*.

To see more of this author's work, go to http://faithwriters.com/testimonies2.php.

SO THAT
By Stacie Snell

The brilliant spring sunshine flooded through the hospital window, a stark contrast to the gloominess that resided in the dark corners of my broken heart. There I sat, huddled up in a tight corner next to machines and monitors that sustained the life of my very sick three-month-old baby. Pneumonia had gotten the best of her. Limp and unresponsive, my tiny Sydnee lay there nearing death. After being sedated and intubated for nearly five days, her condition only grew worse with each passing day.

Curled up in my chair, I stared watchfully at the heart monitor, listening for that high-pitched beep that would signify her oxygen saturation had dropped too low. With each rhythmic beep of the monitor, I felt a little more hope slip away. Day after day, I had held on, believing in God for a miracle, but on this particular day, after hearing that her condition had once again worsened overnight, I felt completely depleted; my soul lay as limp and unresponsive as my baby daughter's body.

That morning, friends from my church, whom I define as Heroines of Hope, came to visit. They carried the hope of Jesus with them and always seemed prepared to share a word of encouragement. Choking back the tears, I asked them, "How do you hang on to hope when there's no hope left?"

So That

Neither one of them blurted out the flippant answers many had given me, such as, "Hang in there, honey, she's going to be okay." I knew those answers came from well-meaning hearts, but the hope they were offering was false hope. Truly, nobody knew whether she was going to be okay, not even the doctors.

I needed someone to speak truth to me at that moment. My friend, Kelly, leaned in, firmly grabbed my hand, and said, "Let Him meet you where you are. Pour out your heart to Him. Tell Him you are out of hope, and He will give you what you need."

After they left, I picked up my Bible and prayed. *Okay, Lord, I need hope. I need to know that you see this; that you see what is happening. I need to know that you are taking care of my Sydnee.*

God then led me to Isaiah 40:11 which says, *"He tends his flock like a shepherd: He gathers the lambs in his arms and carries them close to his heart; he gently leads those that have young" (NIV).*

Tears immediately began streaming down my face, and a spark flickered inside my heart. I closed my eyes and pictured Jesus carrying my little lamb, as I stood beside Him, being gently led by my Good Shepherd. My hope for the day was that Jesus would carry Sydnee, as He gently led us through the journey. A tiny revival had begun in my heartsick soul– a transfusion of hope throughout my entire being.

For the next few days, we continued to receive discouraging news, but we prayed relentlessly. We seemed to develop a pattern of prayer, bad news, updates to friends and family, and more prayer. The days began to blend as this pattern became as routine as the scheduled vital checks made by Sydnee's doctors and nurses. Yet, in the midst of the mundane and unremarkable, a remarkable God met us daily. While everything else appeared to be stagnant, God showed up with a fresh word and new mercies whenever we called on

Him. His word came to life, and His presence was manifested in ways we had never experienced before.

After two horrific weeks in the PICU, Sydnee made a miraculous turnaround and was well enough to come home. She was on her way to a complete recovery, but as we made the hour-long trek home, I felt as if *I* would now need some medical attention to fix my broken heart. Pieces of it remained shattered after watching my baby suffer, and I didn't understand why God would allow this to happen. The big question that we humans tend to ask in the face of a trial weighed heavy on my heart–*Why?* Why had God allowed my daughter to become so sick after I prayed for my children's health every day? Why would a good God allow any child to suffer? *Why?*

As we settled in at home, I knew the only way to begin to heal would be to go to God with it all. Kelly's words rang in my ears, "Let Him meet you where you are. Pour out your heart to Him...He will give you what you need."

So, I did just that. I went to Him with my pain, fear, and frustration. I released it all. As soon as I finished pouring out my heart and asking Him my honest questions, I heard His still small voice whisper, "So that."

At first, I was shocked. *Could God actually be answering the question we are so often told we will never know the answer to?* I sat in silence for a while, still wondering if I had heard Him right. After hearing it again, I went to my Bible software and looked up all the times the phrase, "so that," is used in the Bible. It turns out that it is used a lot. It appears at least forty-seven times in the context of something bad happening. For the next few hours, God took me on a journey through His Word and gently answered my question. Verse after verse, I asked why, and He softly answered, "So that..."

About midway through the Bible, I began to see the pattern. Everything that God allows to happen in the lives of His children is ultimately for our good and His glory, and all that He does or allows springs from His heart of love. Yet, deep down I still struggled with how God could possibly use sick children for good. Just as I wrestled with that thought, the next verse listed in my concordance took me straight into a Gospel story about a sick child. It turns out Jesus healed a lot of sick children. Suddenly it hit me smack dab in the face. Those sick little ones and their families experienced Jesus in miraculous ways, but it started with a sick child. If those children had been healthy, perhaps those families would have missed the personal encounter with Jesus altogether.

Memories of the last two weeks flooded my mind, but this time they weren't flashbacks of terrible sights or nauseating smells. Instead, I saw Jesus. I saw Him rising up with healing in His wings... (Malachi 4:2); carrying my little lamb in His arms when I was unable to cuddle her myself. He was there lifting me up with His gentle words and fresh mercies and holding my family together as we encircled her bed to pray. We walked through the fire *so that* we could see Jesus in ways we otherwise would have missed. God's love was written all over my Sydnee's story! To Him be the glory!

ABOUT THE AUTHOR

Stacie Snell is a Christian writer and speaker. She lives in Colorado with her husband, Schad, and their two daughters, Skylar and Sydnee. Her heart is for Women's Ministry, and her passion is to share Jesus through speaking and writing.

To see more of this author's work, go to http://faithwriters.com/testimonies2.php

PURPOSE IN THE PAIN
By Jeremiah Creason

A new season of my life began the day my dad died. I remember hearing the phone ring when I already had so much on my mind. In less than an hour, I would be having a CAT scan of my heart. *Why was this happening to me? What exactly was happening to me?* I had so many unanswered questions. When my cellphone rang, I was still looking for a parking spot, and I answered the phone.

The voice on the other end was quiet, "Jeremiah—" my stepmother said, in a whimpering tone. "He's gone!"

My heart broke.

She continued, struggling to get the words out. "What are we supposed to do now?"

Both of us cried, and all our words became muffled by our uncontrollable emotions. My dad was gone, and I was left alone in a car outside the hospital, staring out the window.

A few months before my dad's passing, I began to experience more health challenges. In a few weeks' time, I went from going to the dentist for a toothache to being diagnosed with trigeminal neuralgia, a nerve disorder that causes debilitating chronic pain along a major nerve in the face.

At thirty years old, I have known many people who have had medical hardships, but I never expected it to happen to me. Maybe I was just naïve. I remember sitting in the rheumatologist's office as they asked me, "Are you Native

American? Do you have any medical illnesses that run in your family?" My answer to both questions was *yes*. As it turns out, I inherited the family disorder.

Dealing with the diagnosis of rheumatoid arthritis wasn't easy. Especially as the pain increased and moved throughout my body. Eventually it affected not only my joints, but my lungs and heart as well. The pain was hard to bear at times, so I prayed a lot.

My car became like my personal sanctuary. *God I know you're in control, but I don't know if I can handle this,* I prayed. It wasn't until one day after seeing the cardiologist that I felt like there may be a purpose for all this. I had retreated to my car, shaken up by the ill effects my heart was experiencing, and I received a text from a good friend of mine. "In order for God to use you greatly, He first has to wound you deeply." It was paraphrase of something A.W. Tozer once said, and it was the start of my situation turning around.

Later that evening, I was lying in bed, my mind was at rest, and I was without pain. I thought about a song by Matt Redman called "10,000 Reasons." Feeling the urge to listen to it, I looked up the video on my phone. I had always felt comforted when hearing it, but this time was different. That five-minute-long song felt a lifetime long as the lyrics began to write my future on my mind. As my eyes watered, I sang about having to face what lies ahead. When I got to the part about failing strength and the end drawing closer, the tears streamed down my face.

Before the song was over, I became so overwhelmed that it was as if someone opened the floodgates. I envisioned my life ending at a very young age, and it was the first time that the possibility of my death became that real to me. *This definitely wasn't part of my plan, God, but it doesn't mean that my life is over. You can still use it for good.*

Although I'd trusted God through this season of life, it wasn't until that evening that I completely gave my weakness over to Him. I'd gone through a personal storm, and although I took some damage, I came out on the other side changed. The faith I had, grew stronger. I understood that now, with this life experience, I could be more effective in the lives of other people with similar struggles.

It wasn't long after, that people began coming into my life, and I was given the opportunity to share with them about my struggles. My eyes had opened, and I saw a need that many people have, which before all this wasn't clear to me. Yes, people need prayer, but they also need to connect with others who understand their situation. Who better to do that than someone who has experienced similar circumstances?

I still have my health issues, but the medication I take has made a significant difference in my life. And I have reached a place where I'm genuinely thankful for the course my life has taken and the relationships I've made along the way. Although the direction life may take remains unknown, having a relationship with a God who knows, makes all the difference in the world. God can do all things; I could receive a miraculous healing, a healing by medicine or doctors, or be healed on the other side of this life. As long as I'm living, my faith and my hope remain alive.

"Praise be to the God and Father of our Lord Jesus Christ, the Father of compassion and the God of all comfort, who comforts us in all our troubles, so that we can comfort those in any trouble with the comfort we ourselves receive from God." (2 Corinthians 1:3-4 NIV)

ABOUT THE AUTHOR

Jeremiah Creason is an author and a machinist, who has a passion for learning and teaching. He enjoys investing his time in discipleship and apologetics. He and his wife have two children and live in the Oklahoma City area, USA.

To see more of this author's work, go to http://faithwriters.com/testimonies2.php.

ENDURING DREAMS
By Darlene Free Edmondson

Until age fifteen, I was okay. My three older brothers had taught me how to be a tomboy, and I adored the attention. I relished squishing mud-pies through my fingers, climbing mimosa trees, playing football, and milking our cow, Lady, who produced the yummiest milk for butter and buttermilk in the whole community. Mom gathered us at bedtime and read stories from the family Bible. One particular character named Joseph grabbed my attention because of his coat of many colors and his nickname, *the dreamer*.

But then, my dad died, and I knew I'd never be okay again. He suffered a heart attack while operating a bulldozer. Dad slumped in the driver's seat and lost control of the gears. The machine turned upside-down, and the smokestack pierced dad's chest. He was forty-three. To call this a traumatizing event would be an understatement since a dark vacuum invaded my soul, and I begged, "I want my daddy! I want my daddy!" I can't say how long I stayed on my knees repeating that phrase, but it seemed endless.

A week later, the caretakers shoveled cold dirt onto his casket. As they buried Dad, I tried to bury the whole scene within the recesses of my mind. It didn't work. I thought about him all the time, especially at night. I dreamed of us playing basketball, riding the tractor, baling hay, working in the garden, and swimming in the pond. Pleasant dreams for certain, but morning came only to remind me that he was gone.

I experienced severe loneliness that developed into raging anger against God. I couldn't trust Him anymore. Yet, I remember the day, at age nine when I'd had confidence in Him.

Long before that, on an Easter Sunday night in 1959, the choir tenderly sang a beloved hymn by John Newton called "Amazing Grace." That powerful song pierced my soul like a fiery branding iron. It convicted me of being lost and needing to be found, blind and longing to see.

I'd said, "Hold my Easter bonnet, Daddy; I'm going down front and getting saved. I feel God drawing me, and I ain't putting it off any longer!"

White-haired pastor Samuel Garrett waited as I neared the rustic altar of Opossum Rock Baptist Church in Oneida, Tennessee. Other than my dad, Preacher Sam was the kindest man I knew, and I was born again.

After leaving Dad's grave that rainy day in 1966, I purposed in my heart to put on a brave face—a disguise to mask fear of being abandoned again, never being loved or wanted, not being good enough and *perhaps his death was my fault.*

Ambition became my new best friend. Barreling onward, earning a bachelor's and master's degree, I started, but didn't finish a PhD program, which screamed, "You need help." Each degree left me emptier.

Sure, I desired close friendships, but fear of losing someone again paralyzed my ability to have intimacy with family members or others. This domineering do-it-myself attitude cloaked the real me for three decades. Slogging along, I resembled the fragile tumbleweed—disengaged from rooted foundations—nobody heading nowhere.

Sporadically, a touch of normalcy surfaced, and I began thinking of marriage. I wanted a husband and children. I desperately wanted someone to love, and one who would love me unconditionally. Working at University Hospital in Jacksonville Florida, I stumbled upon a magnificent man, and my outlook donned a ray of hope.

Yep, happiness was mine, including a white-picket-fence (literally) and anything else my princess heart demanded. What more could I want? I had a great life, a husband, and four precious children. Still, dissatisfaction nagged, and the search for meaning continued. I began to understand I needed healing in areas of rejection, mistrust, and abandonment.

Finally, a new dawn of reckoning appeared. Mom went home to glory. Even though my dad's passing immobilized me, Mom's death catapulted me toward inner wholeness. Coming full circle, I accepted the depth of God's limitless love, grace, and compassion.

These needed mercies had been there previously, but I was too hurt to accept them. Father God's acts of boundless love reached the uttermost regions and were out of all proportion to my sin, shame, or grief. It was humbling in every area of my being. Intruding on my whole person left me with no choice but to let my Abba Daddy love me. True love. Real love. No-strings-attached love.

That's it. Jesus loved me. This I knew. I'm beginning to nudge closer to God every day. I'm not afraid now because He calms my worries, replacing them with His gift of peace.

Last year, while I slept on the couch, I dreamed Jesus walked into my living room. Around three in the morning, He appeared, a perfect gentleman with a shining, bronze-like face. His humility mesmerized me, and I felt deep peace. He didn't speak, but He knelt, stretched out His hands and prayed over me. Mom sat at the foot of the couch, and I called to her, "Mom, Mom, it's Jesus!"

She couldn't hear me.

Then I hollered out to my husband, "Lee, Lee, come see Jesus!"

Immediately, my darling husband of thirty-four years bounded to my side, "Darlene, are you alright?"

I whispered, "Yes, I'm okay."

ABOUT THE AUTHOR

Darlene Free Edmondson lives in Georgia with her husband Lee. They have four adult children. Darlene loves goat-feeding, dog-walking, chicken-egg gathering, ducks swimming, deer-sightings, bird-watching and cat-napping.

To see more of this author's work, go to http://faithwriters.com/testimonies2.php.

LETTING GO
By Katherine Kane

It was daft things that Patrick* and I had in common–a mutual love of Wensleydale cheese, long walks, and a dry sense of humour. We also complemented each other well. Patrick, being several years older than I, was very assertive; I was much more diplomatic. Patrick emboldened me, and I was a calming influence on him. Soon, he became like a second father and mentor to me, as well as godfather to my older son.

For Patrick, an only child and bachelor, his friends were his family. A devout and mature Christian, he often reminded me of the proverbial mustard seed–the tiniest seed of faith that grew into something capable of supporting many others (Mark 4:30-34). He was the friend who supported me through the spiritual crisis precipitated by the ending of my first marriage. I couldn't face church and struggled to pray alone. Two or three times a week, Patrick and I would talk and pray together via the phone. Despite how I felt, Patrick's reaching out to me was the proof I needed that God had not abandoned me.

In time, I met Alan. Before long, we were planning our wedding. Patrick wrote and read the prayers at our wedding service. At the reception, he joined in the dancing and fun, cracking jokes as usual about hoping to meet a rich widow one day.

Monday evening rolled round, my usual time to catch-up with Patrick. Very early on in the call, Patrick's exhaustion was audible. Yet his fatigue was eclipsed by excitement as he relayed how he'd heard from a friend that he'd lost touch with and their plans to meet up.

Thursday morning, I was out Christmas shopping, still on cloud nine from the weekend's wedding. My mobile trilled. When I answered, Dad said, "I need you to come over to the house straight away."

Worried, I headed to my parents' home. As soon as I entered, Dad had me sit down. "I'm so sorry, Katherine, I'm afraid Patrick has died."

I sat at the kitchen table, stunned, staring through the rising steam of a mug of tea. Its warmth could barely penetrate the cold numbness of shock. All the elation and joy of my wedding, four days before, seemed a lifetime ago. Apparently, Patrick had suffered a sudden massive heart attack on Tuesday around lunchtime. *If I could have Monday's conversation again, what would I say that I didn't? Could I have brought myself to end the call?*

Part of me was sure that, soon enough, he would call me and explain it had all been one big wind-up. But I realised deep down that I was clutching at straws, trying to hide from having to face reality. Gut-wrenching sadness, unanswerable questions, anger, feelings of powerless and bereft all became regular companions.

Yet, even in this terrible pain, God's handprints were recognisable. Patrick's great fear was to end up alone in old age. He died young, but surrounded by friends and knowing he was loved. The timing of it had not escaped my notice; having been the vessel of God's healing and love throughout my recovery from a broken marriage, Patrick had watched me move into a new phase of life. At least my last memory of him was of him at his happiest.

Over and over in my head, I heard the words, *"Well done, good and faithful servant...enter into the joy of your master" (Matthew 25:21).* This hope was the only thing that could prise open the grip of grief's jaws around my heart, the evidence of a loving God in control, the only salve for when grief bit hard.

Going to the funeral was impossible due to the needs of my children. In any case, I could not have equated my vivacious friend with being in a wooden box.

Three years later, we were driving through North Wales near the retreat centre that Patrick had considered the nearest thing he had to a home. He had often promised to bring me here, but died before we could arrange it. We rang ahead to find out if we could call in. By chance, one of the Brothers who had been close to Patrick was available for a short time.

I could see what attracted Patrick to the stunning location. Although he loved the people whom God had called him to serve in the city, his natural preference was for peace and quiet. I pulled into the driveway and parked opposite the retreat centre building. The beautiful chapel building astounded me. The conversations Patrick and I had shared years ago in which he had described it all to me came alive in my mind. Straight away, I could see why he had wanted to bring me here so badly.

We were greeted warmly and shown around the centre. I saw the library where Patrick had spent many hours meticulously archiving. I smiled as I recalled how this task, which would have driven me crackers, gave him such a sense of fulfilment. *God really knew what He was doing when He led Patrick to this place! Thank you, Lord, for blessing me with this incredible friend.*

Because this Brother had such a limited time to spend with us, I knew that God intervened to make this meeting happen. If we had arrived earlier or later, I would have missed meeting the man who was close to Patrick. I am so grateful because sharing memories of Patrick helped me to begin the healing process.

Sitting in the pews of the chapel, I could picture Patrick here, finding spiritual sustenance in this oasis. Here, more than anywhere, I felt a strong sense that he had found peace. *He was my close friend, Lord, but Your child. You and You alone knew what was right for him. Knowing him, I bet he's already organised my 'welcome home' party. Just keep me strong until that day finally comes ...*

Six years on, there have been many happy events in my life that I wish Patrick could have celebrated with me. There have been many dark moments where I've wished I could just pick up the phone and talk through it, as once I could. There have been times where I've wondered, *What would Patrick advise me to do?*

Deep down, I know the answer to that question. His response to virtually every problem I shared with him was "Well, my dear, I shall pray about all of this." Those words that I heard so often are permanently etched into my memory, and now they remind me that I can take whatever's on my mind straight to God, who will always hear and respond.

God has helped me accept that He had a different plan for Patrick than the rich widow he semi-seriously joked about. I don't know why Patrick left this life so prematurely. But I do believe that God, as his loving Father, had His reasons; reasons that, right now, I would be incapable of comprehending. Perhaps I'll understand once I get to Heaven. But for now, the best way I can thank God for bringing Patrick into my life is to be the kind of friend to others that he was to me.

* Name changed.

ABOUT THE AUTHOR

Katherine Kane lives in the UK with husband Alan and three children. Besides writing, she loves walking along the beach with her dog.

To see more of this author's work, go to http://faithwriters.com/testimonies2.php.

MY JOURNEY THROUGH DEPRESSION
By Milly Born

Oh God, I don't know if this is working. I slouched in a chair and tried to forge my floating thoughts into a prayer. My exhausted mind escaped into nothingness. My body craved food. It was day three of my first fast. My husband, Jan, had asked me to join him in a liquid fast to add power to our prayers for healing of old hurts and for direction for the future. I expected to soar to higher levels of spirituality, but I was dragged down by intense headaches and waves of nausea instead. *Can't I just go to bed and sleep until tomorrow when we can eat again?*

I desperately needed to hear from God. *Talk to me, Jesus. I know You are with me. I also know Jan loves me. But I don't feel anything. I just feel barren, Lord. And ashamed. Why can't I be a merry-hearted Christian?* I was in the midst of a depression.

Only a year earlier, my husband had been elated when I finally accepted Jesus. Until then, I'd been living as an atheist, always trying to be in command of my life. I had been convinced that I was a good person and relied on my own capabilities to attain wisdom and happiness. God had no place in my life. I had believed that only weak and stupid people needed some sort of god because they either wouldn't or couldn't take responsibility for their own lives.

But over time, my convictions wilted under the weight of reality. I still didn't grasp the essence of mankind—or myself—in spite of my study of psychology. My fruitless quest for unconditional love had filled my heart with self-pity and my mind with unanswered questions. *Don't I have the right to be happy? Why do I exist? Do I even have a purpose at all?* My ever-increasing workload only wore me out.

Amid the confusion and despite my pride, God pursued me with His love and grace–relentlessly–until I could deny Him no longer. *I thank you Jesus, for not giving up on me. But why am I so dejected now, so listless? Help me understand.*

In the months following my baptism, my joyful journey as a new Christian faltered as issues from the past unexpectedly emerged. As if that were not enough, I entered early menopause, just when I was desperately hoping for a baby. I descended into a spiritual desert, becoming blunt and bad-tempered. Pain, anger, and bitterness consumed me, taking a toll on our marriage.

Thirsty for a solution, I absorbed the words of television preachers. I followed every piece of advice and prayed every prayer for deliverance. I read the Bible daily and claimed every Biblical promise of love, peace, and joy for my life. I delved ever deeper into my heart to identify the source of my misery.

Nothing is helping, oh Lord, not even fasting worked. God, what am I to do? Speak to me, please. I sighed as I flipped the pages of my Bible.

Then I felt it—a nudge towards the book of Psalms. The gentle pushing stopped when I reached Psalm 78—a lesson about how the people of Israel kept wandering around in the desert after God had freed them from slavery in Egypt.

Why did they travel through the desert, God? Did you want to test their faith and faithfulness? To see if they were worthy of their destination?

No, the journey through the desert was simply the route to the Promised Land, a journey in God's presence. He had set them free and was guiding them to their destination. They were grateful at first, rejoicing in their deliverance from the Egyptian pharaoh. I imagined the relief they must have felt was similar to what I had experienced when Jesus rescued me from the world's demands—and my own—to perform and conform to other people's standards. I was on my way to my spiritual destination.

However, the Israelites fell back into their habits of grumbling and complaining, reverting to old idols, and feeling lost and miserable. God saw it happen and confronted them, but they didn't repent. Instead of trusting Him, they despaired and questioned His faithfulness with every problem they encountered.

Like the people of Israel, I had my share of setbacks on the journey. Instead of continuing to trust in God's presence and purpose, I reverted to my old ways. Even though the Holy Spirit was living within me and guiding me, I nurtured past wounds and mourned present imperfections.

God's people kept wandering in the wilderness and never arrived at the next phase of God's plan for them. God wasn't punishing them; they simply wouldn't have been able to enter the Promised Land and face the challenges awaiting them until they were able to depend on and totally trust Him.

Trust Him. Suddenly, I saw it–my pride, my resentment, my bitterness—all stumbling blocks that prevented me from going forth into the future. God loved me, but He wouldn't remove my self-created obstacles if I didn't trust Him. *I'm so sorry, God. My walk with You has been a fiasco. Forgive me. Help me. Show me the way out of the desert.*

Again, He nudged me to read His Word. *"O God, you are my God; earnestly I seek you; my soul thirsts for you; my flesh faints for you, as in a dry and weary land where there is no water." (Psalm 63:1)*

Overwhelmed, I realized that Jesus knew exactly how I felt. When I read verse eight, *"My soul clings to you; your right hand upholds me,"* it was as if I heard Him speaking directly to me. *Cling to Me. Only My presence can quench your thirst. Let go of the idea that you have to control your life, solve every problem, and answer every question. I am the only solution, the only answer.*

Tired of introspection, I reached out to Him. *Search my heart, God, and show me what to do. Restore my soul.* I surrendered completely. I repented of the negative feelings I had nourished. He started healing and transforming me. In the weeks that followed, anger gave way to peace, bitterness to love, and despair to gratitude. I marveled as a quiet, restful joy returned. Jesus was more than my Savior – He was my Lord. I followed Him out of the desert of depression and into the highlands of hope.

Now, nine years later, I humbly thank Him for the many blessings in my promised land. My marriage revived, a child arrived. He gave me a vision and a ministry. He enables me to serve Him for His glory.

Every morning, while listening to my favorite worship songs, I seek Him. He's always there. Every day, I confess my own helplessness and put my trust in Him alone.

I still encounter challenges—I still struggle—but never alone. My Lord goes always before me, making a way. He gives me strength and courage; I cling to Him.

ABOUT THE AUTHOR

Originally, from the Netherlands, Milly Born and her husband, Jan, gave up their business careers and moved to the South of France. Later, they were drawn to Italy, and in 2004, they moved to Umbria. They are the parents of an adoptive daughter and pastor a Christian community.

To see more of this author's work, go to http://faithwriters.com/testimonies2.php

ON BEING A PERSISTENT WIDOW
By Dee Hardy

It is hard to say when I reached my lowest, and there have been multiple times. My worst episodes flared up when Satan's darts and deceiving words discouraged and weakened me so much that I told God that I hated him. I remember pleading with God. "Why do you hate me so much? Can't you see what's happening?"

God didn't answer.

"I can't take any more of this. I thought you took care of widows. You took my husband from me. Haven't I suffered enough?"

God remained silent.

"Okay, now, I realize You do hate me!" I sobbed as I screamed, shaking my fist toward the heavens. "You're destroying my dreams, my happiness. What kind of father does that to His child? You let my enemies win while I suffer humiliation. Everything is breaking. I can't take it anymore." By this point, I felt hysterical and hoarse from screaming for several days. "Yes, You hate me, so I hate You back. Please just let me die. There's no place for me in this world anymore. Please let me die."

I am not proud of these conversations. Not many people will admit to being angry with God, much less admitting hatred. My beleaguered eyes saw a loving Jesus and a punishing God. How did I sink so low?

My world went dark during the wee hours of December 1, 2008. I changed into a different person in the seconds that it took for my daughter to say, "He didn't make it." What seemed important before, no longer mattered, and a huge wound spread through my chest—a wound that never heals. The first year of grief is always the hardest, and my first year as a widow was a nightmare. Along with the pain of loss, came problem after problem after problem.

It felt like our home had gone into hibernation during the last few years of my husband's life. Not long afterwards, it woke up, screaming for attention, demanding repairs from a grief-stricken widow ill-equipped to deal with unscrupulous contractors—some who were not the slightest bit hesitant to prey on the vulnerable. God sent several contractors who were decent and of good character. I prayed that God blessed them and their families. They never knew how much I appreciated their honesty and kindness.

There were many repairs. The kitchen floor soon needed replacing. Then the well pump broke, which left our country home without water. Not only did the water heater break, but it also flooded the kitchen and laundry area, resulting in long hours of mopping and cleaning. It seemed as soon as I fixed one thing, something else would need repair. I had plumbers and electricians in and out of the house. Then I had to replace the central air conditioner. Of course, there were the normal maintenance bills, but there were also costs for additional repairs and updates for increasing my home's value. In a desperate attempt to pay the bills on just my income, I tried to refinance the mortgage loan twice at a lower interest rate. I also had to repair and maintain the car, truck, and lawn mower. My depressed state of mind produced self-destructive behavior that led to more debt, adding to my burgeoning problems.

I can almost pinpoint the day my downturn began. The loan specialist, who handled my second attempt at refinancing, called me to say the appraisal came in too low—twenty thousand dollars lower than it did with my first attempt with another mortgager. This news came at the worst possible time—the first anniversary of my husband's death—a day full of pain all by itself.

During each crisis, the devil used it to try to convince me God hated me. I'd been through hard times before my husband died, but I don't believe I ever experienced spiritual warfare, at least not on this level and intensity. At times, I became so angry, I stopped praying, or at least I thought I had. I talked to the Lord all day, not in a good way, but the communication was still there.

The vehicle that aided in my slow ruination was when I took my eyes off God. The fuel for this horrific journey came from one source: deep, intense grief. Satan used that opening to work on my thinking and convinced me that my troubles were God's fault.

I drifted away from church, isolating myself from people who live what the Bible teaches–another drastic mistake. I believe those folks wanted to follow the advice Paul gave to the Thessalonians almost two thousand years ago. *"Therefore encourage one another and build each other up, just as in fact you are doing." (1 Thessalonians 5:11 NLT)*

However, people couldn't encourage me or build me up because I wasn't there. I felt worthless, inadequate, and unloved, even by my Maker, thus opening the door further to attacks from Satan. I stopped taking care of my health and appearance, deepening the depression that gripped me. The poison seeped into every area of my life, draining me of all hope, while Satan used it to convince me that God allowed it because He was punishing me.

Feeling like all hope was gone, I knew nothing happened without God allowing it; however, I couldn't understand how a widow's destruction could ever glorify his name. In my tortured mind, I pictured God turning His back on me, setting me beside the road as if I was a sack of trash.

I was wrong. Troubled, discouraged, and stressed-out, I couldn't feel the strong hand of the Lord on my shoulder when the tears flooded my eyes and soaked my cheeks; my mind felt too muddled to comprehend there was a purpose for my pain. Even though I thought God and I weren't speaking to each other, I realized that I had never stopped conversing with Him, but I couldn't hear His voice any more. The anger and discouragement plugged up my ears.

Like Daniel in the lion's den, I began to look at God and not at my problems. Suddenly, I related to Peter when he took his eyes off Jesus and began to sink (Matthew 14:30); I was drowning because I refused to focus on the Lord.

Today, I still encounter problems; some of them are the same ones, others have developed recently. In Luke 18:1-8, Jesus taught the Parable of the Persistent Widow. He said she did not give up, and neither will I. A friend recommended that I keep a gratitude journal to remind myself, although burdened and struggling, I still have much to thank God for every day.

The grief, discouragement, and Satan's attacks led to my fractured thinking. Jesus said, "Do not ever give up, never stop praying, I am with you always." On His words, this widow clings, staying persistent in prayer as He instructed, trusting Him, and knowing He is control of my difficult situations. My Lord will right the wrongs and restore what I have lost as only He can.

ABOUT THE AUTHOR

Dee Hardy is a mother and grandmother who resides in Greensboro, Georgia, and works in information technology. She loves reading, writing, and spending time with family and friends.

To see more of this author's work, go to http://faithwriters.com/testimonies2.php.

CASTING BREAD UPON THE WATERS
By Mary Sue Moss

I had always considered myself a second-mile Christian. But this was put to the test when asked to share my house for an indefinite period with my husband's fifty-year-old homeless, underweight, and alcoholic cousin.

I had heard rumors that Dale wanted to come live with us and work for my husband. *Not in my lifetime,* I thought. But Dale did come. After a friendly, "Good morning," to start the day, I mostly ignored my husband's cousin. I accepted him and cooked a little more, but watched mostly from the sidelines. My husband measured out the teaspoons of liquor for two weeks to make sure Dale didn't go into delirium tremens; it was he who talked and listened, and when healing took place, offered Dale a job.

One day, as I walked past Dale's open bedroom door, I noticed yet another reason to add to my growing list of why Dale should not be in our home. I was horrified to see a small smattering of excrement, the result of gastroenteritis, sullying the light gray carpet. Meanwhile, our guest was in the kitchen, washing the breakfast dishes. Two solutions came to my mind: the first, *This was my husband's idea and his relative, so he could clean it up,* the second, *I could give the cleaning materials to the one who made the offending spot and use the opportunity to teach responsibility.*

I chose neither of these options, but instead touched my knees to the floor and started scrubbing. Another unholy thought came to my mind. *If this doesn't come clean, the church's assistance committee will get the opportunity to bless me with a new carpet.*

I kept scrubbing. Unexpectedly, I found tears wetting my cheeks, as I was overwhelmed with love for my Jesus and for the cousin in the kitchen. My Lord seemed to say, *My child, your stiff-necked, stiff-armed welcome policy to this man isn't love. It's wood. All the meals you have cooked, the extra desserts you have fixed, and the special ice cream you have purchased aren't love. They are hay. Your act of willing payments for an increased grocery and water bill isn't love. It is stubble (1 Corinthians 3:12).*

I felt so guilty about my unloving attitude. But God also used this to show me a touch of His mercy, reminding me that if any man's work abide...he shall receive a reward (1 Corinthians 3:14).

Okay, Lord, for heavenly rewards, I can do this.

Dale's presence was good for a few chuckles. One day, he announced to my husband, "I have a bone to pick with you about your wife. Can we speak in private?"

The two of them stood in the dining room, which hardly was secluded from me at the kitchen sink. Dale said, "Your wife has a bad habit. She won't put the twistee on the bread bag. You know, she just folds the bag and tucks it under–with no twistee!"

I found the complaint about my housekeeping quite amusing coming from this man, who, before coming to live with us, had slept on the streets and was fortunate to get a piece of bread with his bowl of soup in the food line. What was my husband going to say? Trying to contain myself, I waited for an answer.

My husband redeemed himself not only to me but also to Dale, "There are two principle people in this house: my wife and I. We make the decisions here."

I was itching to add my two cents-worth, *and we don't major in the minors*, but restrained myself.

I wish I could say that Dale turned away from his liquor and found productive employment. He didn't. By summer, he was back to his life on the streets. He lived for three years in a motel on his newly acquired social security checks. He died of alcohol poisoning at just fifty-nine years of age.

Dale's son and his wife flew to Iowa from New York for their father's funeral, and they thanked my husband for what he had tried to do for their incorrigible father. It was good to see them as a strong family that was not following the path that Dale had chosen.

The case was closed, or so I thought. The lessons learned would have been good enough if the story ended there. But it didn't; the Lord had more in store for our family.

We had no contact with Dale's son for six years, but we heard that his family was moving back to Iowa to live on Grandpa's farm. That Grandpa was the man who had grieved over his alcoholic son, Dale, and had been the father figure for his grandchildren.

I met up with Dale's daughter-in-law at a bridal shower and she asked me how my husband was doing. She had heard that he was battling cancer. It told her that we're doing okay with the cancer stuff, but what he needed was a good business manager. The current bookkeeper was going to quit. The quitting wasn't the problem, but the books and the business records were in a shambles.

"Seriously? Your husband is hiring?"

Two weeks later, Dale's daughter-in-law plowed into the books for my husband's business and corrected a year's worth of errors and neglect. She was everything that Dale couldn't be. But if Dale hadn't been in need of a home twelve years prior, and my husband had not literally guided his sick, emaciated form through our door, we probably would not have found his daughter-in-law. My husband had cast his bread upon the waters for six months and it returned twelve years later as balanced books at the year's end. I was privileged to ride along on my husband's shirttail to learn that God's ways are best.

ABOUT THE AUTHOR

Mary Sue Moss and her husband are part of an agricultural community in Iowa. She is a RN with twenty-seven years in geriatric nursing followed by fifteen years as a teacher in a small church school. Fourteen grandchildren and a weekly newsletter keep life in retirement busy.

To see more of this author's work, go to http://faithwriters.com/testimonies2.php

MOURNING INTO DANCING
By Julie Berry

"You have turned for me, my mourning into dancing..."
(Psalm 30:11)

I walked into the church on a Monday morning. I could smell the coffee, hear the laughter and feel the excitement as staff and volunteers gathered to start the week. This was my dream job, full-time ministry. Normally, I would have been right in there with them but not today. Today was my last day. No one knew but me. Looking at the sea of smiling faces, only one thought raced through my mind. *I can't do this anymore.*

Months of despair had enveloped my heart and left me hopeless. I muttered an excuse to the secretary and walked to my car, numb to the core. I drove straight home, went in my bedroom, and took the cap off a bottle of sleeping pills. I had no more tears left to cry. There had been too many nights of sobbing, begging God to make the pain stop. The pain couldn't be cured with an aspirin or a Band-Aid; it ran so deep and felt so anguished that it caused a constant, physical ache. I was ready for it to end...permanently.

Suicide. Seriously? I was on staff at a church. I had been on staff with Campus Crusade for Christ. *I'm spiritually superior; right. Become a Christian and life is perfect.*

People at church constantly asked, "How are you?"

I'd nod my head, plaster a fake smile on my face, and say, "Fine." They'd keep on walking, but I wasn't fine. I wanted to tell them. I wanted to run after them, grab them by the arm, spin them around, and scream, "I am not fine!"

With one last gasp, one last plea for help before I crossed a line that I could never come back from, I called my best friend. She had established a relationship with my Christian counselor. She called him, and he phoned me. On the inside I was screaming, *Help me!* but on the phone with him, I was defiant. "You can't stop me!"

Much to my surprise, he could and did; it involved law enforcement.

Within twenty-four hours, the doctors admitted me to a psychiatric ward on suicide watch. They searched through every inch of my luggage. I sat on the bed in stunned disbelief. *How did I get here? How did this happen?* They forced me to attend group therapy with drug addicts, alcoholics, sex addicts, and abuse victims. Not wanting to be there, I slumped down in the chair, somehow thinking I could make myself invisible. It didn't work. Instead, I disappeared inside myself and walked around like a zombie.

After a few days of intense sessions with a psychiatrist and a therapist, who were both determined to keep me from sliding into the dark abyss that had begun to swallow every dimension of my life, I began to make progress.

The horrible pain that had a vice grip on my heart began to heal. First, I had to admit it; I had to say it aloud. Words that were so inconceivable to me that I could not even form them in my mind were now pouring out in a waterfall of confession. "I want to be loved." The single concept that had wreaked havoc in my life was contained in those five simple words.

While growing up, my parents had never spoken the words, "I love you." My emotionally absent father and alcoholic mother had done the best they could in raising my siblings and me, but the lack of that simple phrase had caused a huge, gaping hole that I desperately tried to fill in any way possible.

I had graduated as valedictorian from my high school and with honors from college while obtaining my Bachelor's Degree in Music Education. I had a successful career, many friends and a great life and when God called me into full-time ministry, I felt I had arrived.

After being hired at my church, I fell to my knees one night, and in a moment of spiritual snobbery, I prayed. *God, if there is any garbage in my life that is keeping me from being as close to You as possible, please remove it.* I stood up, went on my merry way to the next church function, and never looked back.

A year later, I was in the hospital, diagnosed with acute depression.

This smart, popular, young woman was a mess–co-dependent, manipulative, and filled with fear. Basically, I was an emotional black hole.

Until God brought me to the place where truth and love were poured into me, I hadn't realized just how messed up my world had become. I just hadn't known.

I walked into the psychiatric unit, broken and ready to give up on life. I danced out two weeks later, a new creation. For the first time ever, I knew who I truly was, and still am, in Christ. I am redeemed; I am whole, and He loves me. However, I wasn't done; I continued counseling for a year. Seeking God, I studied His Word and wrapped myself in truth. Voices no longer told me that no one would ever love me or that I wasn't good enough.

Two years later, a wonderful man got down on one knee and asked me to marry him.

I answered, "Yes, but..." I hesitated because I didn't want to marry him if I was looking to have him fill a need in my life.

When I got alone later that night, I immediately fell to my knees, wept and poured out my heart and my concern to God. He spoke to me in that quiet voice that brought immeasurable peace into my soul. "Julie, marry him! You are not trying to fill a void in your life. You allowed *Me* to meet that need for you by bringing him to you."

I had come a long way.

Twenty years and three boys later, I'm surrounded by four men who love me more than I ever conceived was possible sitting on that bed the first day in the psychiatric ward.

A couple of years after my battle with depression, I went for a walk in my neighborhood. I reflected on all the healing God had brought into my life. I'd met so many people along the journey, and I wondered, *Why me, God? Why did You heal me?*

Once again, I heard the quiet voice of Jesus. "Because you asked me to."

I was confused at first, and then, the memory washed over me like a giant flood, taking my breath away. That night, I had prayed in the height of spiritual arrogance for God to remove the garbage in my life. I thought I had arrived at the Christian pinnacle of life, but He knew differently. He removed the garbage and so much more.

ABOUT THE AUTHOR

Julie Berry lives in Pearland, Texas with her husband and three teenage boys. She has a Bachelor's Degree in Music Education and teaches private lessons at her studio. She has written scripts and served as writer/editor for her church.

To see more of this author's work, go to http://faithwriters.com/testimonies2.php

THE WORST OF SINNERS ~ THE BEST OF GRACE AND MERCY
By Steve Bragg

"And the grace of our Lord was more than abundant, with the faith and love which are found in Christ Jesus. It is a trustworthy statement, deserving full acceptance, that Christ Jesus came into the world to save sinners, among whom I am foremost of all. Yet for this reason I found mercy, so that in me as the foremost, Jesus Christ might demonstrate His perfect patience as an example for those who would believe in Him for eternal life." (1 Timothy 1:14-16 NASB)

At seven years of age, my grandmother took me to see *The Ten Commandments* by Cecil B DeMille. I was spellbound by Moses standing on a cliff, ready to open the Red Sea. My continued prayer each night for many years was, *God, use my life like you did Moses'*.

My grandmother was an ordained Four Square Preacher. However, Grandma had a drinking problem that overtook her life and ministry. She fell from ministry and left our lives at the request of my mother. Grandma came to see me late one night at my bedroom window. I believe I was aged ten at that time. She gave me a Bible and said this book would be my life. She talked about the dedication to the Lord of the first-born male child. I am the first-born. She prayed for me with power and conviction that I would serve the Lord. I never saw my grandmother again.

My grandmother, mother, father, and stepfather all drank heavily and had morality issues. As I grew with no guidance in faith, I was lost to the world of drinking, drugs, and immorality.

The Lord had heard my prayer as a young child to serve Him, and I believe He honored the dedication prayer of my grandmother. At age twenty-seven, I found the Lord and immediately entered Bible College. In college, I learned the Bible well, but had not understood how the power of God could transform my life. I was able to keep the drinking, drugs, and immorality at bay. Soon after graduation, while in my first preaching ministry, the strongholds of these sins overtook my life once again. I had learned the theology of God's Word, but missed its life. I was still dead in my trespasses and sin. Like my grandmother, I fell from the ministry. I lost everything including family, ministry, reputation, and church.

In my fallen state, I embraced the darkness. Flames of lustful desires burned in my heart and could not be quenched. Indeed, I became one of the worst of all sinners. There was not much that I did not experience.

After thirteen years of wandering in darkness, sin had destroyed me. All that was left of my life was in ruins. There was only heartache and the pain of an empty, unfulfilled life. I had longed to serve the Lord – I still longed to serve the Lord – but had thrown that away. I concluded that my sins were too great for Him to restore my life into His service.

Finally, in desperation, I fell to my knees and asked God if He could forgive me. My only hope was His forgiveness. I asked, if possible, if I could have a little happiness in this life.

To my amazement, God took the broken pieces of my life and not only forgave me, but also restored me into a powerful ministry that I could never have imagined. My heart was broken, but God would use my broken heart to save me from the ravages of sin. I was to discover the depths of not only His forgiveness, but also His grace and mercy. Like the apostle Paul, I was to declare that if God could forgive and use the worst of sinners, me, He can forgive and restore you as well (1 Timothy 1:15-16).

One night, I went to a church service. It was a church that did not know about my past. I sat in the back, ready to make a quick exit after the service. I did not want to answer the probing questions that would embarrass me by revealing I was once a pastor, but had fallen from the ministry.

At the end of the service, the pastor started talking about Communion. He talked about our Lord's sacrifice of His blood and life for my sins. He spoke of the resurrection and the hope of eternal life. I wanted to run out the door, but I was glued to the chair. Tears were shooting from my eyes as the Communion symbols of the bread and juice came to me. Never did our Lord's Supper mean so much to me as then. When I arrived home, I said to the Lord, *You arranged that just for me, thank you*!

I wanted to go to church regularly now. The Lord had blessed me with a new wife, also a Christian. I found a church and met up with the pastor over a coffee. I wanted to tell him who I was: a fallen pastor. Partway through my story, he stopped me and said that he also fell, but God had restored his life and ministry. His words to me changed my life: "God loves you, Steve!" Oh, these words were like cool water to a man dying of thirst.

For several years, this pastor and other mentors taught me how to live with God. They helped me back onto the path of life in our Lord! My restoration into His service was slow. First, I led a Bible study, then a life group, and then I became a board member, and finally an elder. Just a few years ago, my restoration was completed as I was ordained a pastor.

In 2005, to illustrate the Parable of the Talents (Matt. 25:14-30), I was given a $100 and asked to invest it in the

Kingdom of God. I prayed that God would show me how to use the money, and if I could be a part of whatever blessing it became. At that same time, my wife's sister in the Philippines was praying for a church in her remote community. I enlisted the help of others, and soon that $100 became Grace Chapel. We attended its dedication in 2006.

For the next few years, my Lord continued to draw me into a deeper relationship with Him. In 2011, my family and I moved to the Philippines as missionaries. Now, in 2014, we have twenty-three new churches in remote areas of the Philippines. We have many care programs in the name of our Lord Jesus. These ministries of love provide regular feedings for malnourished children, school scholarships for less fortunate children, health programs, support for pastors, clothing programs, and, most of all, the hope of our Lord Jesus and His saving mercy and grace. Many lives and communities are being transformed with the loving care of our Lord.

Today, my life is fulfilled and overflowing as my prayer as a seven-year-old boy is being answered. For each day, I see the proof in my life that *"The Lord will fight for you while you keep silent"(Exodus 14:14 NASB)*. Amen!

ABOUT THE AUTHOR

Pastor Steve Bragg is a missionary serving in the Philippines. Thirteen years after falling from the ministry, he began his incredible journey with our Lord Jesus Christ. God has not only forgiven him, but also restored him to an extraordinary life walking with God. It is a miraculous story, a story of grace.

To see more of this author's work, go to http://faithwriters.com/testimonies2.php

HAUNTED BY HURRICANES
By: D. Katy Tyler

The storm came in without much warning. Troubling signs had been on the horizon, yet I was unaware that, on this day, my life would become splintered, much like the aftermath of a hurricane.

After an afternoon of teaching, I hurried home with my three young children. As I started dinner, the boys were playing in the backyard, and my husband was still at work. My daughter came into the kitchen, sat down in the old rocking chair and whispered softly,

"Mom, I need to ask you something."

I responded cheerily, "What do you need to ask me?"

"Come over here, I don't want the boys to hear me."

As she nestled in my arms, abruptly she asked, "Why won't Daddy stop coming into my room to watch me dress? I told him I don't like it, but he keeps doing it anyway."

Shivers of alarm ran along my spine. Almost thirteen years of marriage had taught me that my husband had little regard when it came to my expressions of discomfort, especially in our most intimate moments. He flatly stated that I owed him whatever he wanted; I was his wife.

My adored children were unaware of this aspect of our life; it was private. Abusive verbal remarks were hurled at me in the silence of the night, when no one else could hear. Threats of physical abuse were becoming a nightly ritual.

Confused thoughts tumbled around in my mind constantly. I did not want to see our lives torn apart. I did not want a divorce.

We were a family heavily involved in church. On Sunday mornings, we looked like the perfect family, spiffed up and polished fine. What would everyone think if they knew, what would happen if I left? And, what did God think about all this? There seemed to be no simple answers, only many tangled questions.

I took a deep breath and asked, "Does Daddy do anything else to make you uncomfortable?"

"No," she said as she squirmed out of my arms.

I sat unmoving. My spirit knew; this was the beginning of something and it wasn't good. My daughter was a beautiful, delightful six-year-old with a whimsical, albeit headstrong, personality. Lately, she had grown increasingly defiant and unruly; I was completely puzzled by this change in her behavior.

When confronted, my husband denied my daughter's comments while making this statement, "I always knew someday you would accuse me of being a child molester."

Up to that moment, I had never, even in my most disillusioned times, thought such a thing about him. In spite of the misery I had suffered, I did not believe him capable of harming his own daughter.

When he threatened me with inconceivable physical harm, I knew our home was no longer safe. We fled to my brother's house in another city.

The next few weeks brought drastic changes. My daughter's initial question was simply the first cracklings of an enormous, shocking tempest. She'd thrown out a little truth to see if I would believe her; once I did, more revelations followed.

Friends provided a safe haven for the kids while I hired an attorney, found a new job, and secured a place to live. My family helped settled the kids into a new school. Incredible friends provided the kids with much-needed fun and adventures, giving them a temporary distraction from their pain and confusion.

Tumultuous months followed, filled with multiple court dates, counseling sessions, detective investigations, and involvement by the district attorney, child protective services, and finally, an analysis of our entire family by a court psychologist.

My daughter and I had to talk to all sorts of strangers about personal, private things. Fortunately, a complete physical exam by a highly trained specialist revealed that my daughter was never fully raped. According to a well-qualified counselor, she was being prepped for such an event; we had just stopped it in time.

Everyone, except the judge, believed my daughter had been violated. Only after a court psychologist stated without reservation that it was his professional opinion my soon-to-be ex-husband was a pedophile did it become legally settled that my children did not have to spend time alone with their father.

Life went on as I endeavored to function in the frenetic world of every day.

Yet, I wanted to hide away until the pulsating pain stopped as I endured lonely nights with a heart that was twisted into broken pieces. Tears flowed as I asked, "Why?" not with the whine of "Why me?" but rather, with the cry of a spirit broken, unable to comprehend the shattered dreams, unrelenting agony, and unfathomable guilt. How could a mother not know? Where was God while it was happening?

My faith faltered. The pastor at my old church believed my daughter made the whole thing up; he told me I was wrong to leave my husband. Why should I go to church, wouldn't every pastor think the same way? I was completely unable to reconcile my circumstances with the image I had of a loving, protective Heavenly Father. I could recite Bible verses. However, they felt like lofty platitudes. The formerly strong cord binding me to my Savior was stretched tenuously thin. I felt it would soon break and hurl me into even darker places.

A chance meeting with a wise pastor was the first step toward healing. He explained that, over the years, he had seen naïve pastors innocently believe men in their congregation incapable of such egregious conduct and, as such, they became convinced there were other explanations for these situations. He also reminded me that God does not approve of such actions and He weeps along with the brokenhearted.

Next, I began to realize that while God hears and answers our prayers, He does not manipulate mankind. God is not a genie to whom we relay our wishes and, magically, they come true. Each man has a free will to make choices and sometimes those choices are evil, hurting innocent people. In my case, God allowed me to learn the facts before they proceeded any further, but after they had established a pattern of conduct that the courts found unacceptable.

Eventually, a crossroad emerged. I could proceed into the dark abyss of bitter anger and unrelenting despair. Or, I could walk toward the light of God's peace. Another wise counseling pastor listened a lot and talked a little. My spirit began to mend as I realized only Heaven is free of sorrow. Earth hands out disease, dilemma, and destruction in varying degrees—at unexpected seasons. As I read and interacted with others who had successfully negotiated through their painful experiences, I began to comprehend that Jesus had been walking alongside, each and every day.

Although I did not forget the shattering pain, I was able release the matter into my Father's care. He then started changing the disaster into something of great worth. My faith became stronger as I understood that He sustained me through my darkest hours. Scriptures took on new meaning as the wisdom embedded in them became clearer.

Finally, the peace of God, passing all my understanding, had prevailed in my spirit.

ABOUT THE AUTHOR

D. Katy Tyler has published a collection of short stories, a variety of articles, devotionals, and a historical novel; she is currently working on its sequel. She is involved in her local church, specifically in music. Katy enjoys antique-hunting and long walks with her husband and dog.

To see more of this author's work, go to http://faithwriters.com/testimonies2.php

TUESDAY AFTERNOON
By Dot Hannah

My husband and I were carefully unpacking as we scurried around our hotel room on that fateful Tuesday afternoon. We were on a short, relaxing trip and, for now, all troubles had drifted away from our busy minds as we prepared to become fancy free the next few days. We could not have expected how frantic the day was about to become, and how the unexpected and uninvited was about to strike hard and fast.

It was early afternoon when the call came. The concerned voice of my daughter's husband bluntly explained that she had been critically injured in a car wreck. One moment Kelly was driving to pick up her children, the next being air lifted by helicopter to a trauma center. She had experienced her own personal earthquake, and now life and death were quarreling over her. Immediately, a new mood erupted, taking possession of me and overwhelming my spirit. I could not believe this torturous nightmare that we were now facing. *What if I never saw her again?* I wept, I prayed. My heart was pounding and my chest tight with anxiety. I asked God to step in to calm my emotions, and, immediately, my strong faith in Him vaccinated me from the turmoil.

The sun had set and the afternoon turned black as we drove home, the longest four hours of my life. *Would I arrive in time? Would I lose my precious daughter, who is such a large piece of my life? Would my lovely grandchildren lose their mother?* It was out of my hands. I had to pray passionately and trust the outcome to God. Then the words came into my mind, and I whispered them in the darkness. *"Be still, and know that I am God..." (Psalm 46:10a KJV)*

We arrived and rushed to our despondent son-in-law's side in the intensive care waiting room. A traumatic brain injury, a broken back and ribs, a ruptured spleen and damage to both choroidal arteries were the most serious injuries. Her body was shattered like pottery. Would life ever be the same? Would she ever be able to live a normal life again? The battle she faced would be the toughest she had ever fought, but I took great comfort in the fact that she was indeed a fighter.

An outpouring of love and kindness from friends, family, and fellow Christians supported us in the turbulent days ahead. We watched Kelly suffering much pain, but knew the strong and enduring arms of Jesus delivered her through the worst of times. Because of her brain injury, she encountered a welter of despairing confusion, which caused her to ramble and say irrational and bizarre things. It was with true eagerness that she awaited our visits as days and weeks passed. Taking it slowly, for she was in no condition to hurry, we encouragingly spoke to her about her children so she would look forward to getting well and going home.

One month and two days later, my vivacious daughter left the hospital. Kelly had been knocked down but not knocked out. The Lord healed her at the very threshold of death's door, with the help of her excellent physicians. She suffers short-term memory loss and headaches, but she copes and lives a normal life. There is inexpressible happiness and gratitude in our hearts. It has confirmed my faith that, in all circumstances of life, the Lord is my sufficiency.

I believe this accident was God getting involved in her life, and mine, in a dramatic way. This life-jolting experience was a way to awaken decisions that change the course of one's destiny, and given me a story of God's goodness to share. For me, this experience of suffering has led me to view the ordinary differently, and learn the art of enjoying every small detail.

This experience made me weigh up the pros and cons of living life for God's larger purposes. But His calibrated and precise scales reveal to me that there are no cons. Indeed, He has shown me what appears to be disastrous can become the birth of commitment and a new, full life. I hope and pray His guidance will give Kelly the ability to make prudent choices, and, if she yields, He will polish and shine her like a precious gem.

Hard times may come again and again, turning my world upside down. But I have a history with God–a living God, who is worth believing and trusting. And I will hold fast. Bleak circumstances have never hindered Him. He and I make a majority, and He cares deeply about all the events in my life.

"Be still, and know that I am God: I will be exalted among the heathen, I will be exalted in the earth."
(Psalm 46:10 KJV)

ABOUT THE AUTHOR

Dot Hannah is sixty-one-year-old wife, mother, and grandmother. She is the church's bookkeeper and works as a bookkeeper for her husband's business. She loves to write and loves the Lord.

To see more of this author's work, go to http://faithwriters.com/testimonies2.php

COMING TO FAITH SECTION

HE GIVES HIS BELOVED SLEEP
By Phyllis Sather

If there is a God, He certainly doesn't care about me. My thoughts tormented me as I gathered my bottles of tranquilizers and a new bottle of wine.

After a year of searching, I still couldn't prove there was a god. I had read every book I could find on the topic, but no one seemed to have an answer that satisfied my heart.

The nightmares about placing my child for adoption continued to haunt me. No matter how many pills or how much alcohol I consumed, I still woke dripping with sweat. The nightmare was always the same–someone took my daughter away from me. The reason for removing her from my custody also remained the same each time. I had placed my illegitimate son for adoption, and the person in my nightmare used that as the excuse for ripping my daughter from my arms. I would wake up filled with dread, certain I'd never see her again. Ten years of nightmares, and all I wanted was to sleep without waking up full of fear, and then beating myself up for what I considered an unforgiveable sin. I felt so ashamed that I had never told anyone about my firstborn child and my choice to give him away.

Diane was the one friend I had who seemed to have it all together. Even after her husband left her for another woman, she was able to go on with her life. I had been attending church with her because that seemed to be the biggest difference between us. Unfortunately, I didn't find any comfort there. One night, after hours of drinking alone, I called Diane. "I'm going to kill myself. The pain is too much. I can't bear it any longer."

After listening sympathetically she said, "I think you've talked with me enough. You need to talk to God. Ask Him to give you something that will be meaningful only to you." My jaw dropped when she hung up on me.

I'm not sure what happened after that, but the next thing I knew I woke up in bed feeling disoriented. Shaking my head, I was stunned that the nightmare wasn't what roused me. It was something else–but what? I looked at the clock—six o'clock—AM or PM? Squinting, I realized it was evening; however, the last thing I remembered happened sixteen hours ago. I was totally sober and hadn't had the nightmare. My mind raced as my friend's words echoed in my ears. "…something that will be meaningful only to you." The one thing I needed was uninterrupted sleep. *Only a powerful God would know that. If I slept without dreaming, God must be real.*

As my feet hit the floor, I started praying. *God, I'm not really a bad person. You won't need to do much to change me.* Suddenly, I stood still. *How do I know I need to change unless God is telling me so?*

My heart pounded as my mind raced. Before I knew it, I ran to the bathroom and dumped all of my prescription drugs into the toilet. Next, I raced to the kitchen, started grabbing the bottles of alcohol, and dumped them down the drain. When every pill was gone and every bottle empty, I dropped into a chair, trembling.

There is a God. Those words pounded through my mind repeatedly. *There is a God; there is a God.* My heart felt like it would burst. *There is a God–and He cares about me!* I dropped my head into my hands and sobbed.

Oh God, whatever are You going to do with a thirty-year-old single mother who is addicted to prescription drugs and alcohol, smokes non-stop, sleeps with her fiancé, and is dishonest?

I called Diane, who came over and helped me repent and commit my life to the Lord. We discussed my drug and alcohol use, and we both knew that I would experience withdrawal. She assured me that she would be there for me and would get me medical help if it became necessary. Days went by, and all I felt was joy bubbling up inside me. Jesus had removed my addiction.

After that, going to church was a life-changing event. The liturgy came alive to me, the words echoing the joy I felt in my heart. I had told my fiancé of my new relationship with the Lord, but he wasn't interested. In fact, he seemed almost jealous when he said, "If you go to church on Christmas, our relationship is over."

I didn't believe he truly meant it, but when we returned to his house after the service the door was locked, and he wouldn't answer. It was over.

I remember sitting at my kitchen table, thinking that I should be sad about the end of our two-year relationship. Instead, a grin spread across my face as the love of Jesus filled my heart. I knew Jesus had removed him from my life, and I was at peace.

A few months later, a friend invited me to a Christian conference adding, "Oh, you'll need a Bible." That was the first time in my one-year walk with the Lord that anyone had mentioned that I should be reading the Bible. Thinking I would only use it that week, I chose a five-dollar paperback from the clearance table.

One night during the conference, I realized that I'd given my entire life to Jesus. *What if it wasn't real?* If only I had been reading the Bible like the speaker said, God would be able to give me a verse that would reassure me. I glanced down at my open Bible and read the words, *"You will show me the path of life; In Your presence [is] fullness of joy; At Your right hand [are] pleasures forevermore."* *(Psalm 16:11 NKJ)*

It described my life with the Lord perfectly, and all of my doubts flew away. I became a student of the Bible and my little paperback version soon needed to be taped together in many places.

Over the next few years, I went back to where I had placed my son for adoption and found peace with all the demons that had haunted me for so long. I received forgiveness and was able to forgive myself.

The Lord continues to use His Word in my life to restore what was destroyed. This verse continues to bring new meaning to my life: *"It is in vain that you rise up early and go late to rest, eating the bread of anxious toil; for he gives to his beloved sleep."* *(Psalm 127:2 RSV)*

ABOUT THE AUTHOR

Phyllis Sather is an ordinary woman serving an extraordinary God. She and her husband of thirty years, Daniel, have three children: Emily, Rebekah, and Eric. In addition to writing a regular column for a magazine, she has published several books, including, *Purposeful Planning*.

To see more of this author's work, go to http://faithwriters.com/testimonies2.php

OUT OF THE BROKENNESS
By Maureen Hager

With a heavy heart, I quickly packed our van with a few essential belongings. Less than six months ago, Viggo* was released from prison. He lied to me when he promised to leave the Demons of Darkness motorcycle gang in exchange for a life together. The NYPD had issued a warrant for his arrest, and now we were on the run. A quick and discreet escape was essential to safeguarding our freedom.

At twenty-six years of age, I dreamed of fleeing from the lifestyle and control the gang imposed on my life. Silently, I masked my anguish and got behind the wheel of the van. I was driving across the country, and soon, my life would change forever.

My parents divorced when I was a young teenager. My mother left us in search of a better life. Consequently, my father had the task of caring for three children. He was not prepared for this responsibility and, being the oldest child, some of the burden of care rested on me. It left me with an overwhelming emptiness in my heart. I sought escape from the pain I felt by numbing myself with drugs.

In spite of all I tried to fill the void in my heart, I could not find satisfaction or love. When I met Viggo, I thought I had finally found the family I longed for. The gang offered me a promise of excitement, abundant drugs, and a sense of belonging. Instead, I became Viggo's property, and I was ordered to do whatever he required of me.

In the evening hours of a warm October night in 1977, we arrived at a house in the suburbs of San Antonio, Texas. Upon entering, I found myself in the midst of a gang war between the Demons of Darkness and the Sons of Lawlessness.

Six nights later, in the early morning hours, the house was quiet. Everyone was asleep except for Viggo and me. When our dogs started barking, Viggo headed to the back door to let them in. I walked to the front bedroom of the house. I had planned on lighting some candles, but I couldn't find any matches. Despite being warned not to turn on lights at night, I flipped on the light switch to quickly search the room. I could hear the dogs running towards me.

Unknown to us, three Sons of Lawlessness gang members stood outside the house, armed with M16 rifles. I was standing in the doorway, facing the front windows, and silhouetted by light when the shooting started. I had reached for the light switch with my left arm, and when the first shots were fired, I felt a fiery sensation in my left forearm that had covered my heart.

The impact of the bullets threw me face down. Before I hit the floor, another bullet lodged in my right thigh. My left arm had been blown apart, and the bone in my leg was shattered. The shooting continued; I could not move. The bedroom blinds lay ripped open; glass and bullet casings covered the floor, and my flesh was splattered on the ceiling.

When the shooting stopped, Viggo ran into the bedroom and dragged me into the hallway, despite my protests to stay where I was. "Stash all the drugs and guns," Viggo ordered, gesturing to the others in the house. In a few minutes, the police and paramedics arrived.

Inside the hospital's ER, the police were demanding answers. "Who shot you? Was it your husband?"

While the ER staff jabbed an IV into my arm, a nurse shoved a clipboard in front of me with insurance papers to sign. I was in shock, shivering, and in intense pain. The room was crowded with doctors, nurses, and technicians, yet I felt totally alone.

Hours later, I awoke in the intensive care unit, surrounded by machines beeping. My right knee had pins surgically inserted into the bone; my bandaged leg hung elevated with weights attached to immobilize any movement. My left arm was covered in plaster. An IV needle was taped to my right hand. I had lost a lot of blood, and needed several transfusions.

My doctor touched my shoulder to awaken me and bent down to talk, "Maureen; you have been seriously injured, but you will live. Your injuries will require you to spend the next year of your life in rehab." He went on to say, "In a few days, you will need an additional surgery to stabilize and repair the damage to your leg. I'm not sure if I can save it, but I will do my best." After a reassuring smile and a pat on my shoulder, he left the room.

I was sure God was punishing me. As I lay in bed, motionless and silent, it occurred to me that all my searching for love and acceptance had brought me to this place of hopelessness. The pain and suffering were constant reminders of the uncertainty of my future.

For the next six months, I was completely bedridden. Eventually, when my femur did not fuse together, in another attempt to fuse my shattered bones, the doctor wrapped me in a cocoon of plaster from my chest down to my ankle.

Months later, still in the body cast, Viggo dropped me off at a hospital located in a neighboring state. Once again, he fled from the police; I never saw him again. I was consumed with shame, fear and anger. My family had abandoned me. I was alone and isolated from everyone and everything that was familiar to me.

My body cast was cut off, and a surgeon fused the bones in my leg together, using a bone fragment from my hip. A metal rod placed in my leg added strength during the healing process. My leg was now permanently two inches shorter.

In desperation, I called my father. He came and drove me to a hospital in New Jersey. Lying in the back of a station wagon on my way home, I felt some relief from the loneliness. Determined to start a new life, I severed all ties with the gang.

My injuries required a full year of intensive rehabilitation. During this time, a friend invited me to attend a baptismal service at her church. I did not believe a church would be a welcoming place for me, but I agreed to go because of the transformation I saw in her. When I heard the testimonies of others, the good news of the Gospel filled my heart with hope.

All of my own efforts to start a new life had failed miserably. That night, I asked Jesus to be my Lord and Savior. I am so grateful that He had a better purpose and plan for my life.

In time, the Lord healed the bitterness and the anger I held in my heart. Sin had its consequences, but He set me free from the drugs and the lifestyle I had been living. He put a new desire in my heart to follow Him.

Today, I have the family that I longed for. The Lord blessed me with a godly husband and two precious daughters. Accepting Jesus as my Savior, transformed my life. Not only do I have eternal life with Him, but also I have His love, His joy, and His peace to walk in victory each day. I am enjoying His provision as He prepares the path before me.

*Names of person, gangs, and locations have been changed.

ABOUT THE AUTHOR

Maureen's journey through emotional, spiritual, and physical trauma is a testimony of the power of God's transforming love. Her message of hope and healing out of brokenness has impacted women of all ages. She and her husband live in Western North Carolina.

To see more of this author's work, go to http://faithwriters.com/testimonies2.php

FINDING THE KING OF THE JEWS
By Sylvia Maltzman

My mother and father were American Jews who had lived through the anti-Semitism in this country during and after World War II. They had seen signs in store windows and hotels that read, "No Jews or dogs." They knew Henry Ford had to be sued before allowing Jews to work in his factories. No wonder that they felt threatened by Gentiles and nourished a seething hostility toward Christians.

However, they weren't proud to be Jewish, either, and once my elderly paternal grandfather stopped pressuring my dad to put his children through Hebrew school, I never entered a synagogue or received religious instruction. My parents hated talking about God, but they did mention that we Jews were somehow the chosen people, and Christians, who were bad people, hated us and wanted to hurt us. I remember hearing, "Watch out for those Gentiles because they are all out to get you."

I couldn't understand this and asked myself, *Why do they hate me? What did I do to them?*

Mom and Dad never explained the difference between a Jew and a Christian, but they warned me to be ready for trouble.

The one time I remember going to the synagogue with my parents, a stranger told me about God. I couldn't have been more than four years old; I was asking questions and getting restless while waiting for something to happen.

My parents sat in the wooden pew, chatting softly between themselves, ignoring my questions. I squirmed a little, trying to get comfortable against the hard seat.

I asked, "Where are we? Why are we here? What are we supposed to be doing?"

Instead of answering my questions, my mother shook her head and scowled at me as she raised her eyebrows. As soon as I saw that look, I knew I'd better sit still and shut up or I'd be in big trouble. Just then, an elderly woman in the pew in front of us turned around and started answering my questions. "We're in a synagogue."

I couldn't pronounce the unfamiliar word, so I asked, "Well, what are we doing here?"

She smiled at me. "We came here to talk to God."

Furrowing my brow, I leaned forward to hear more about this stranger she called God.

Patting my arm, the woman answered my unasked question. "God is the One who made Heaven and Earth and everything you can see. Why, he even made you."

Immediately, I felt something stir in me, like a little light bulb turning on. The kind stranger went on, "In every synagogue, there is a small reminder of the Everlasting Light that had once burned in the Temple." She pointed to the tiny orange bulb flickering softly near the ceiling above the altar. When she mentioned God, I had immediately associated that light with the feeling in my chest.

I needed to know more about God, but my parents refused to explain, so I did the next best thing. I went out into the yard and spent time with all the things that God had made, especially a little lantana bush, which produced flowers in many different colors. Since I wasn't allowed to talk about our religion, this was the only means I had of getting closer to God or learning anything about Him.

Later, Dad bought a small black and white television, and I discovered that if I woke up early in the morning on the weekends, I could tune in to any of the three Miami stations and watch programs about God before anyone else woke up. I didn't learn much because a lot of what they said didn't make sense to me, but I kept watching because that was my only source.

One day when I was nine or ten, I turned on the TV to see two men in a stark little room laughing and smiling. I had never seen anyone so happy in my entire life, and never on TV. They were talking about many different things, but each of them kept coming back to one phrase. "Jesus is the King of the Jews. Jesus Christ is the King of the Jews!" Then they would laugh and talk about something else for a minute, but they kept repeating those words, as though they couldn't help themselves, as though they felt compelled to say it.

Now wait a minute, I thought. *I know about the president, but I've never heard of a king in America. All I've ever about Jews is that Christians don't like us. The only time I hear the words, "Jesus Christ," is when someone is cursing.* I felt very confused. Then, all of a sudden, I had a startling thought. *Even though everyone picks on us and hates us, if we Jews have a king, then it means everything is going to be okay because the king is going to help us. The king is going to save us!*

Because I was a good reader, I knew my vowel sounds; therefore, I had never put the words *Christ* and *Christians* together. After all, the long *i* sound in *Christ* was not the same as the short *i* sound in *Christian*. God's dragnet snatched me up with a vowel!

I didn't know it then, but I had opened my heart to Jesus the Messiah. In that moment, I received Him, and He saved me. It wasn't until many years later, however, that I fully understood that, but I knew, then, that I had to find out more about Him. I tried to ask my parents. I knew that God was a taboo subject, but I just had to know more.

In order to minimize the trouble I might get into, I waited for the right moment to ask them. One day, when my whole family was riding in the old Studebaker, I found a long lull in the conversation. I leaned forward, and asked, "Mom, Dad, did you know that Jesus is the King of the Jews?"

They didn't answer me. I thought that maybe they didn't hear me, so I asked again, much louder. "Mom, Dad, did you know that Jesus is the King of the Jews?"

A look passed between them, and it wasn't a pleasant one. I think they had tried to prepare themselves for such a moment, and now it had come. Mom turned to me, and quietly, forcefully said, "You can't believe in Jesus. You're a Jew."

I didn't dare contradict her, but I didn't understand.

She continued, "It's not possible for you to believe in Jesus because you're a Jew."

I was more confused than ever. *I am a Jew, and I already believe. How is it not possible?*

Later on, Mom warned, "If you believe in Jesus, you will no longer be Jewish." No one ever refuted the fact that Jesus was the King of the Jews; they only stated that I couldn't have anything to do with him.

It took many years for me to straighten out that confusion, but with God's help, I learned how to be a Jewish Believer in Christ. God's incredible grace reached me with the tiny, candle-like letter, *i*, and sparked an eternal belief.

ABOUT THE AUTHOR

Sylvia Maltzman, a Jewish Believer in Christ, has lived in Miami, Florida, for nearly fifty years. She's active in her Messianic congregation, Bet Hesed, and loves to share her faith with others. She has a Bachelor's Degree in English and works as a college English tutor. She shares her home with four cats and a Yorkie.

To see more of this author's work, go to http://faithwriters.com/testimonies2.php.

FIGHTING THE GOOD FIGHT
By Lilly Grace

Even though Dad was fifty-two, ladies still noticed my tall, dark, and handsome father. Dad never blended into the crowd. When he walked into a room, everyone stared at him. People seemed to enjoy being with him, but I believe that he hated himself and never felt worthy of love or attention. Although others appeared to respect him, he had a dark secret; he was an alcoholic. Nevertheless, he taught at Northwestern University, participated in Mothers Against Drunk Drivers, and was Regional Administrator of Highway Safety. When he received his first DUI, he must have felt humiliated.

I remember being ashamed of my dad's alcoholism, as if I had something to do with it or could prevent him from drinking. I longed for the love he gave to others; sometimes I felt like strangers received more love from him than I did. I strived for his acceptance, but he never granted it. I studied my friends' relationships with their fathers. *Are all father-daughter relationships like mine?*

When my father got his DUI, I was twenty years old and was shoved into adulthood, a place I wasn't ready for yet. That night, I heard my mother screaming. I ran up the staircase in two leaps and dashed into the master bedroom, decorated in luminous, white and green wallpaper and fluffy brown-speckled shag carpeting. I stopped short when I saw my dad lying on top of the king-sized bed. I pressed my hand against my nose and mouth as I scrunched my eyes tight. "What happened?" I felt my knees grow weak.

Grabbing my arm, Mom tugged me away from the grisly scene. "Don't look!"

Too late, my eyes had already engrained the vision of my father with a gun in his hand into my mind forever. Dad had committed suicide with a shot to his head. The whole scene had a white cottony ring around it and began to move in slow motion; I saw a ghost trail from each movement.

My mother kept screaming, "Hon, what did you do?"

Next, my oldest brother ran in, shouting, "Call 911!" There was no saving Dad; he was gone–gone forever.

The funeral procession went on for miles. Government officials came in from Washington; Highway Administrators from the surrounding states arrived in large, black glistening cars. It looked like the president had died.

One of my neighbors said, "You must be so proud of your dad."

Snorting softly, my shoulders slumped. *We can never forgive each other now nor ever fix things. He just left; how could he do that?*

It would be hypocritical of me to say that my dad was the only one with an addiction to hide. I began to dabble in dangerous drugs right before my dad's death, and my drug of choice was cocaine. At first, I only used it occasionally, but soon I snorted every weekend, and before I knew it, I began using it daily. I would lie, steal, and cheat to get what I needed, and I didn't worry about anyone who got hurt in the process. I would wake up in the mornings with terrible headaches, but at nighttime, I'd start all over again.

One morning, I woke up in my badly painted yellow room with blue carpeting. The room seemed too big. I had always been afraid to sleep by myself in it. My imagination would run wild with all the scary things that could hide in the shadows. That day, I awoke with a horrible headache. I stumbled, and then, crawled into the shower to run water over my face. The bright bathroom with its beaming white walls, white shower tile, white toilet and sink, and the glaring white floor with blue trim didn't help.

On the plus side, I met Jesus in that white bathroom. While in the shower, I lost my eyesight and was in complete darkness for thirty minutes. Sobbing, I started to panic. I flushed my eyes with cold water, yet I could see nothing. I've heard people say that you're not supposed to bargain with God, but in my desperation, I shouted, "Please don't do this! If you give me back my sight, I promise I'll never do drugs again."

Collapsing to my knees, I bowed my head and prayed. *Dear Jesus, I now understand that you are my Lord and Savior, my magnificent king, my Father in Heaven.* When I opened my eyes, my eyesight returned.

Although I knew I was saved, part of me was afraid to announce it to the world. *If I acknowledged God completely in my everyday life, what did that mean? What would be required of me? I can't be a nun; it's too late for that!* I felt dazed and confused, and the enemy worked hard to keep me that way. Satan convinced me that if I truly were a child of God, I would not have done so many bad things. He had me trying to find something or someone that would fill the void and take the hurt away.

I cried out to God. *I know You love me, so You must be on my side, right?* Then, the Holy Spirit convinced me to have a good, long heart-to-heart conversation with God. To be honest, it was unlike anything I had experienced before. The sunlight coming through the window made my living room warm and cozy as the sweet smell of lilac filled the air from the bouquet sitting on the coffee table. Kneeling, I prayed once more. This time, though, I asked Jesus to come into my heart and forgive my sins. It was an instantaneous transaction. He took all my sin, nailed it to the cross, and gave me life in return. Crying, I sat with Jesus, basking in the warm sunlight. This time when I left the room, I knew I was a child of God and that He was definitely on my side.

Jesus took me from darkness into the light with His transforming love. The growing process had begun, and I embraced it with all honesty. I remember talking to God. *I don't know how to pray, will you teach me? I want a pure heart, with no selfish motives. Teach me to pray so that it will be pleasing to You.* God showed me what I needed to leave in the past so that I could grow and become the person He created me to be.

He showed me that my dad was just a man and he didn't mean to hurt me. Through the grace that God extended to me, I was able to do the same for my dad and forgive him. My earthy father and I had a hard relationship, but my Heavenly Father and I are, well…Heavenly!

I kept my promise and never used cocaine again; that was twenty-seven years ago. I thank God every day for saving me and adopting me into His family. Life is not perfect, but I have peace and freedom in Christ, and I will keep fighting the good fight. *"You will seek me and find me, when you seek me with all of your heart." (Jeremiah 29:13 NIV)*

ABOUT THE AUTHOR

Lilly Grace and her husband of twenty-three years, Dave, and their sons, Chris and Kyle, call Indiana, USA, home. Lilly enjoys reading, writing, cooking and traveling. As her children head off to college, Lilly dreams of visiting every state and becoming a full-time Christian writer.

To see more of this author's work, go to http://faithwriters.com/testimonies2.php

BEAUTY FOR ASHES
By Pamela Couvrette

Concealed by the darkness of night, I hurried to the gathering located off one of the busiest intersections in my city. Down an unremarkable street, in a nondescript building, in a forgettable room, held a motley group of strangers. Proceedings began, and as we formed a circle, I started to relax. *This doesn't seem so unusual*, I thought. Then, my eyes fell upon the object, which tattled of the aberration of the meeting–the athame–a ritual dagger. I shouldn't have been surprised to see this. After all, I was in a gathering of witches.

Only a couple of years prior to this night, I believed our lives held no more merit than the life of an apple. We are birthed, and then fall to the ground and die with no purpose except to survive. How did I get from atheism to Paganism? For that matter, how did I get from Paganism to Christianity?

In my youth, I never searched for God or the meaning of life. I loved philosophy and pondering the human condition (outside of theology, of course), but eternal matters were of no matter to me. I remember asking a family member, "Do you believe in Heaven?"

The response was, "Only if there's a hell."

Despite my lack of a theology degree, I sensed this answer wasn't really an answer at all. That was the extent of my deep and longing soul search for God. Louis C.K., the comedian, said, "Ever wonder what happens after you die? Actually, a lot of things happen. Just none of them include you." That summed up my thoughts regarding the afterlife.

Therefore, during my formative years, I was an atheist. Since the theory of evolution was widely endorsed, I never thought to question if it was true. The biblical alternative seemed ludicrous. How people could accept the notion that women were created out of the rib of a man as truth, was beyond me. I didn't know why people kept clinging to religion, believing in the fairytales of the Bible. Weakness? Gullibility? I thought Christians just had a fear of death and wanted to believe in a heaven. All I knew was that religion wasn't for me.

By nineteen years of age, I developed chronic pain in my hands and arms. By age twenty-two, I had exhausted all the avenues of conventional medicine in hopes of healing. It was then that a popular television host promoted a New Age book, and despite my skepticism, I hoped it might deliver insight to my situation. I devoured it, and my worldview shifted. I realized there was an alternate, invisible reality–a spiritual realm. I read more New Age material and sought likeminded people. I learned there were many unconventional healing methods and soon I was involved in *reiki*, crystal healing, astral projection, witchcraft and many other activities. You name it; I did it. I researched Buddhism, Hinduism, Pantheism, Wicca, but never Christianity. I was more apt to believe in fairies and leprechauns than in this man named Jesus who lived thousands of years ago. The only Bible I had was the Witches Bible. I viewed Christianity as the weakest of any belief system and definitely devoid of any power. I concluded it was just a bunch of rules and traditions for people who were feeble minded.

I continued along this path for five years, until the age of twenty-seven. I was happy with my belief system and entranced with the myriad of mystical experiences that occurred in my life. Then one night, I was on the phone with a new friend who simply said, "God, Jesus, and the Bible–it's all true." BOOM! That's all it took. A missing piece slid into place. I knew the truth! I could not deny my Creator–the true Creator of everything. The one true God had graciously revealed Himself to me. I instantly disposed of all my Pagan material, and I was drawn to study the Bible and apologetics (defense of the Christian faith). There was extensive evidence for the claims of Jesus, accuracy of the Bible, and creationism, which I didn't know existed.

While this new knowledge was exciting, the most important truth was that I needed Jesus Christ as my Savior. I did and said things that are against the moral code. Our conscience tells us what is morally right and wrong. That's God's law, and I've broken it many times–which makes me a sinner. Just like any good judge who demands justice, God will punish whoever breaks His laws. Unlike our finite jail sentences, God's jail, Hell, is eternal. Gratefully, Jesus paid for my offenses when He died on the cross. It's a free get-out-of-jail card, so to speak, but just like any gift, if you don't receive it, it's not yours.

My presumptions about Christianity were incorrect. It's not about a bunch of rules because we can never earn God's favor on our own. Christians don't have a fear of death because they know–as I do now–that through Jesus Christ, their eternal life is guaranteed. All those years I scoffed at their ignorance was really my own.

When I think of God's mercy and how He freed me from all the deceptions, it brings tears to my eyes. I still have chronic pain, but I believe it has been a gift. Not only has God used it to bring me to Him, but also He has given me great comfort and joy while in agony, and I would not know these riches and gifts without it. While my priorities were centered on a successful career, the most important thing in my life now is pointing others to Jesus, so they too can be forgiven and have eternal life. I used to mock those who spoke of Jesus. Now I can't stop speaking of Him. If He can forgive me, He can, and will, forgive anyone who comes to Him.

ABOUT THE AUTHOR

A former atheist and New Ager, Pamela is passionate about encouraging Christian women to contend for their faith and rightly interpret Scripture. She loves to laugh and aspires to be hilarious.

To see more of this author's work, go to http://faithwriters.com/testimonies2.php

I WAS A COVERT HELLION
By Linda Gage

I was a thirteen-year-old girl. Frustrated by blaring music from a party on the other side of the wall, I tossed around in bed. Oh, how I wanted to be out there. Instead, angry and cursing my nineteen-year-old brother, I'd been banned to my room. He was in charge, and it was his party because our single mom supported us by taking a better-paying job away from home.

His parties were full of drinking, smoking, dancing, and drugs. Smashing my ear against the cold wall didn't help me distinguish any of the voices. When the laughter and chatting finally subsided, I got dressed and snuck out. Only two guys remained in the living room. One slouched in a corner smoking a joint, and the other changed the album on the stereo and beckoned me over to him. He was cute, older, and paying attention to *me*.

I sat on the floor near him. With slurred speech and acrid liquor breath, he asked me if I wanted *to have some fun*. No one had to tell me what that meant. I jumped up and ran outside.

On the patio, more partiers lingered, but they were too self-absorbed to notice me. One of my brother's friends had a plastic bag and gold smudges around his lips. I had seen this before. Staggering, he sprayed more paint into the bag, covered his mouth, breathed deeply, and toppled to the ground.

How stupid. Yes, I really wanted to be out here, though not to sniff paint. His high was not my high.

My youth had been spent within an arm's reach of alcohol and drugs among other inappropriate teen activities. I had friends who regularly smoked pot, cut school, drank alcohol, had sex, and shoplifted. I was different. I watched while they smoked marijuana during the school lunch-hour, stood look-out at the mall for their five-finger discounts, and invaded many of my brother's parties as a spectator. Friends tried to convince me to join in, but these activities were not part of my rebellion. My high of choice was even closer than arm's reach.

Fifteen years later, I was in church with my husband at my side and a new baby in my arms. Life seemed perfect. The pastor explained how Jesus is the Son of God. I smiled to myself. Dad had sent me to Sunday school; Mom took us to church on Sundays. I already knew about Jesus. Yet, on this Sunday, something was different.

"God's only Son was sacrificed for your sins," the pastor said.

I already knew Jesus died on the cross. Still, something about the message this Sunday was different.

"Because Jesus rose from the dead," the pastor said, "and because he is alive today, you can have a personal relationship with him."

I could have a personal relationship with the man I had seen hanging on the cross?

God stirred and awakened my heart. I was propelled to the altar, knelt, bowed my head, and prayed, *Thank you, God, for sending Jesus to die for my sins. I do believe that Jesus rose from the dead. Please, can I have personal relationship with Jesus?*

These words poured out without understanding—his ways are not my ways.

Some years after the day I'd asked Jesus for a personal relationship, I was in church again: a faithful wife and mom of two daughters we sent to Christian school. I was also a Sunday school teacher, a helper in church youth group, and a regular attendee of Bible study. Life seemed perfect. As usual, I sat upright in the pew with pen and paper in hand to take notes.

A man named Jim was the guest speaker. He was an alcoholic, a drug addict, and a wife beater. He had been arrested multiple times for robbery and killed a man. Then he accepted Jesus and everything changed. Jim was a born-again Christian. His atrocious sins were all forgiven, and now he spent his life telling others of Jesus's saving grace.

As I listened to his riveting story, my tears flowed—not because of his life, but because of mine. I longed to have a story like his. What did I have? I didn't drink, smoke, or do drugs. I'd never killed anyone. Not a spectacular life story. Little did I know, God would soon show me that although my life lacked overt rebellion, I was a covert hellion.

One morning, during a daily Bible devotion, my mind wandered. If only I had a testimony as sensational as Jim's, then I could tell others about Jesus. How would I sound now? "I was a good girl. Then I asked Jesus into my life, and now I'm a good girl." No color there. No dramatic change.

Jim knew the exact day of his rebirth; he knew the exact day Jesus changed his life.

I thought about that day I'd asked Jesus into my heart, and a thought came to me. It was so heinous and horrific, I cringe to utter it. I asked God, *Was that day my rebirth or just a formality for me? I really wasn't that bad. I was good enough, right?*

Like a lightning bolt, instant and illuminating, Jesus's teachings jolted my mind and heart. At that moment, God revealed to me my own atrocious sin. All those years watching others drink, steal, and do drugs, I had lived on a worse high. I was high on a pedestal I'd built for myself, intoxicated on self-righteous thoughts: *I'm a good girl and better than everyone else.*

I looked down on others from a lofty pride-built perch where my life felt perfect. Blinded and convinced of an arrogant lie, I'd believed, *I am good enough to earn God's love.*

Jim's sins were apparent. Mine were hidden, though only from me. In reality, I had done some of the very things I criticized others for doing.

And now, God in his loving kindness was telling me the same thing He had always been telling me—from the cross, through the pastor on my born-again day, and throughout my life: *I love you so much I sent my Son to die for your sins. It's a gift. No one can earn it. Not even you.*

I sobbed and prayed for forgiveness. When was I reborn? I don't know the exact day. But, I do know that God has been with me my entire life. Am I a good girl? Like a recovering alcoholic, who spends the rest of their sober life resisting urges for that one drink, I continue to wrestle against my pride. My life will never be perfect until the Resurrection. But with God's Holy Spirit in me, I will not be blinded by pride again. Jesus changed my mind, my heart, and my life.

Now I toss around in bed imagining the party on the other side—not the other side of the wall, but the other side of this life. Waiting, not in frustration, but in anticipation of the party where I can praise Jesus for eternity and thank God, who invited me to the ultimate party in Heaven.

ABOUT THE AUTHOR

Linda Gage is a Jesus Christ follower, wife, mother, and grandmother. She has a God-given passion to write, and hopes to fulfill His purpose for her life.

To see more of this author's work, go to http://faithwriters.com/testimonies2.php.

IN MY CORNER
By Jules St. Jermaine

Days after I'd learned how to walk, a thump at the front door prompted me to run. The most important man in my life had returned home from work, and I screeched out his name, "Daddy!" I reached for him.

He picked me up and held me.

The next day I raced to greet him. He carried me over to the couch and bent slightly to pick up my pink blanket. He marched me to the overstuffed chair that sat cornered in the dark side of the room. Scuffing sounds against the hardwood flooring caught my attention. His body bowed again; this time he lingered. I watched him place my blanket on the floor behind the chair, and then he lowered me on top of the blanket. He dragged the chair to its original position against the walls, where I couldn't see him, so I waited. He didn't come back.

I approached my Daddy for days until his picking me up transitioned into pointing. Eventually, I dashed to my blanket behind the chair even before he pointed.

By the age of six, I was trained to be in my bedroom with the door shut tight before Daddy could see me. Weekends were long. I was allowed out for meals, chores, or to go outdoors. I wasn't permitted to get a drink unless I asked. Use of the bathroom after I'd been put to bed was unacceptable. Many nights I agonized, holding my urine.

One evening, I heard snoring in the living room, and I made a plan. I slithered on the floor until I reached the bathroom down the hall. Each move I made was deliberate, cautious. I lifted myself up on the seat, balancing with both hands. When I began, as the stream hit the water, it echoed.

My Daddy's sounds stopped! I held my breath, heart racing, anticipating his familiar cruel voice and humiliation. I prayed for God to help me. Daddy let out a few snorts. I hurried to finish.

Quietly, I dragged my body back across the floor, into my room, onto my bed, and clutched my white pillow. Then I felt safe. But my success reverted to fear. I felt I'd been naughty. What if I'd been caught? I came up with the idea to place a jar under my bed so I could relieve myself in the future. I used it for the next ten years.

I prayed and thanked God for keeping Daddy asleep. I asked, "Can you please just bring me to Heaven now? I don't want to live here."

He didn't answer.

When I was seven, my baby sister died of an unexplained seizure. Night after night, I begged God to trade her in Heaven for me. Our priest spoke about how there wasn't any sadness there.

One night I heard a voice inside my head, unlike my own. It said, *When you understand how to get to Heaven, you will die*. This statement may have frightened other children, but not me. I was intrigued. I felt hopeful. I continued pleading.

Around this time, Daddy began bursting into my room whenever he had a bad day at work, or he was angry for any reason. He would yell, lecture, and belittle me, sometimes for up to three hours. I was required to sit up straight, not move, eyes fixed solely on him. To break any of these rules extended the time he'd spend with me. I did clench my fists. Sometimes I couldn't take the stress, and I'd break down crying. My sobbing made him madder.

My teen years were filled with drugs, booze, and cutting. I fell in love with a boy, believing he loved me. He didn't. He hurt me, so I saw all men as hating women as my dad did. I didn't think God cared either, so I quit asking Him to bring me to Heaven. In fact, I stopped talking to Him altogether.

After graduating, I didn't have the grades or confidence for college so I got a job, moved out of the house, and shared an apartment with a friend, who worked nights. At first, I enjoyed feeling free, but it wasn't enough. I was brokenhearted and lonely.

One night I turned on the television for companionship, and we didn't have many channel choices. Billy Graham was on one station, sports on the other. Sports reminded me of my dad with his losing-team tantrums, so I chose Billy.

At first, Billy's southern certainty resembled my dad's, and I rolled my eyes. He began speaking about how Christ had suffered for us. I think it was the word *suffered* that hooked me. Leaning forward, I listened.

Pastor Graham talked about how God had sent His only son Jesus to earth to die a horrible death on the cross for us. He explained how if we accept Him as our Lord and Savior we could go to Heaven when we die. Jesus was the human sacrifice for all our sins! God had decided what it took to get there. We just had to believe Him.

I was amazed; His plan was simple. Before, in church, I'd heard these words, but for some reason, they held no meaning. This time I heard it deep in my spirit as truth, and tears blurred my eyes. I became aware that I had another Father for the first time. He was Father God, and He loved me. He'd always been there, in my corner.

The song "Just as I am" by Charlotte Elliot played. As I listened to the words, I fell to my knees. Tears of peace rushed down my face. My heart filled with an abundance of joy. I accepted Jesus as payment for my sins and asked Him to forgive me that night. I became born again.

Days passed before God revealed to me how I died that night. He never lies. I did die. I died to seeing my world from other people's perspectives. I saw it from God's point of view. My desire to please Him became more important than pleasing myself.

Jesus became my best friend. He's my greatest relationship, my confidant. He understands my problems and my weaknesses. His love is better than human love; it's unconditional; it always exists; it's a knowing.

I still make mistakes; I mess up. During trials of life, I've ached and fought battles with recurring anxiety. With each hardship, I invite God to be in the going-through process with me. He is always faithful to see me to the end, teaching me His ways as I go, and I learn to be more like Jesus.

God helped me to stay focused on his love, not on my dad's putdowns throughout the years. I forgive him for each cruel act because God forgave me for all my sins. During the seven years my dad battled with Alzheimer's, I became his legal guardian and cared for him. I was fiercely protective of him—never unkind. God had filled my heart with my compassion for my dad, and the hurt and anger were gone.

Shortly before his death, his legs wobbled beneath him. I gently grabbed his arm. I helped him sit, and I whispered, "I love you, Dad."

ABOUT THE AUTHOR

Jules St. Jermaine lives with her husband in Michigan. Her love for writing began as a child while listening to her Grandma Mary replaced naughty words with nice ones. Jules is seldom seen without a cup of tea and loves visits from her two grown children, art, and photography.

To see more of this author's work, go to http://faithwriters.com/testimonies2.php.

"GREG! WHAT WILL IT BE HEAVEN OR HELL?"
By Greg Mancini

The voice burst into my mind like a swirling tornado, upending a lethargic town: "Greg, where do you want to spend eternity: in Heaven in My presence or in Hell separated from Me forever?"

Heaven, of course. That's a no-brainer. What a stupid question to be asking me. I was only nineteen years old, and I had my whole future ahead of me. Who was thinking of dying now?

The voice filtered through my mental fog again, "You could die at any time, and you are separated from My presence. Surely at this point in time you will go to Hell."

I was totally confused. Who in the world would be this concerned about where I was going in eternity? I didn't even believe in eternity, let alone God. Like the Lord had confronted Paul on the road to Damascus, the Lord was confronting me about eternity and where I would spend it. (I was not knocked off my horse by a light beam from Heaven.) I moved on, forgetting about this close encounter of the heavenly kind.

One week later, I enrolled at De Anza Junior College, and quite surprised, I saw a former partying friend at the registration desk. We exchanged small talk, but there was something quite different about her. Her face glowed as if she were from another world. She explained to me that she had made her citizenship in Heaven and that when Jesus had become her Savior, He had transformed her life.

"I don't want any of that religious jive," I said. "Come on!"

We talked a few more minutes, and she invited me to come to their church's youth meeting that Wednesday night.

"Yeah, sure. I'll think about coming," I said, but I thought, *Come on, a partier like me going to church to study the Bible and talk about Jesus?*

Never mind, that I was constantly walking under a dark cloud, and I felt like life was not worth living. I'd started sinking into this suicidal mindset immediately after I had been arrested for the first time in Yosemite National Park in August, 1976. Since then, I'd spent every waking moment wishing I were dead. My life was useless, and I had absolutely no hope for a rewarding and fulfilling destiny. I was high a lot of the time, and I was so out of touch with reality that I didn't think much about my hopeless situation. I wasn't going to dig myself out of this drug addiction, either.

I hurried home, ate a quick dinner, and decided to accept her invitation to go the youth meeting. What did I have to lose? I had no direction in life, and I really had nothing better to do. Maybe this youth meeting would give me some hope.

As I was heading out the front door, my mother said, "Greg, don't let these religious fanatics brainwash you into their way of thinking."

"You're dreaming," I yelled back. I hopped into my car and drove to the church. I figured I'd make a cameo appearance, and then I'd be on my way just as fast as I could get out of that religious house.

I walked through the front door of the church, but I had no idea where in the church the service was being held. As I came into the sanctuary, an older-looking gentleman happened to walk by the front door. "Young man, can I help you?" He had the biggest smile and acted like he had known me all my life.

Boy did I feel stupid talking to this strange man. Mustering as much confidence I could, I said, "Ah, I was looking for where the youth hang out."

"Go through those two wooden doors to your left." He pointed to the double doors.

I thanked him and made my grand entrance through the doors. As soon as I entered the dining room, my friend's younger brother stood and waved me over to join him. He looked like he'd been sitting there expecting me to walk through any second. I felt strange being waved to by someone I'd never met before. We introduced ourselves and sat down on the folding chairs. The first question out of my mouth was, "How did you know I was coming through those doors?"

"The Holy Spirit said to be expecting you," he said calmly and smiled.

"You expect me to believe God told you I was coming to this meeting?" Boy, I thought this guy was a real nut to think I was going to believe this tale.

"Yes," he said, and he quickly introduced me to the people around us.

I dropped it real quick. The meeting got underway, and we sang a few praise songs to the Lord. Then we came to the middle of the meeting, which was filled with a Bible study and a time of testifying by the local youth members. The meeting ended with brief bios from all the new visitors. I felt stupid giving a brief description of my life.

Afterward, my old friend from junior college came over with her fiancée, and we had a long, soul-searching chat. Her fiancée told me about his bondage to drugs and how Jesus had delivered him from that awful lifestyle. I had a glimmer of hope that I could finally get some outside help to overcome this drug problem.

He asked me if I was ready to be born again, and I told him I had to think about it awhile—it being a major life-changing commitment.

Later that night, my new friend and I talked more about getting saved. Finally, I agreed to pray to ask Jesus into my life and forgive me of all my sins. I asked, "How do I pray to God?" Her younger brother led me in the salvation prayer, and I asked Jesus to be my Savior.

"I don't feel any different," I said.

"You need to accept Jesus by faith," he said.

We hit it right off, and I drove him home. While we were driving to his house, I sensed a warm feeling inside my body I had never felt before. It felt like two big arms had entered the car and hugged me like I was totally accepted and okay in God's sight. He gave me the knowledge that He had forgiven all my past mistakes, and He loved me just the way I was. I felt accepted and loved like I had never experienced before. Inside my body, I felt innocent, as if I had never committed any crimes or guilty acts. I felt like a newborn baby!

ABOUT THE AUTHOR

Greg Mancini is originally from Sunnyvale, California. He has been married to the same beautiful woman for thirty years, and has two wonderful grown children. He is a graduate of Bethany University and has been a born-again Christian for thirty-eight years.

To see more of this author's work, go to http://faithwriters.com/testimonies2.php.

ONE WOMAN'S TESTIMONY
By Sylvia Hensel

I believed what I was taught as a child, that George Washington was our first president, that Abraham Lincoln freed the slaves, that Jesus Christ died for my sins, and I was to love Him because of that. Even though I learned all *about* these people, I didn't know them personally, and I certainly didn't love any of them. I respected them and believed what I was taught.

I was told that I had better love God, or I would go straight to Hell. That really scared me because I had also learned about Hell. I confessed my love for God, but I wondered, *What kind of love is this that I feel absolutely nothing?* If truth be known, I didn't love God; I feared Him.

Even as a child, what I was being taught seemed impossible to accomplish. I was told I could sin by thought, word, or deed, and it seemed I was always thinking, saying, or doing something wrong. I called out to God, *Surely, You have not created me just to send me to Hell. I can't do this alone.* In my efforts to be good, I felt so defeated.

Throughout my life, I struggled to live by what I'd been taught, but I was an utter failure. I based all of life's serious decisions on what my religion dictated to me, yet my life was a mess. I prayed, but praying to a God I didn't know personally left me feeling isolated.

It wasn't until I turned thirty-eight that I finally met this Jesus I'd been taught about. Through the most horrendous experience of my life, He became real to me. As I faced disaster, I found my church and religious beliefs couldn't see me though the situation. I finally realized I couldn't face life's problems with only a set of rules to go by, and it was impossible to do it on will power, alone.

My problem began when I married at age sixteen—much too young to know what life was all about. It didn't take but three months to realize what a terrible mistake I had made. My husband and I had absolutely nothing in common. However, due to my religious beliefs, I would not even consider divorce. I felt I had given my life away on a whim.

My husband and I worked at our marriage, but I was not a happy person. I turned into a party girl to give a little interest to my life. My dear husband tried to keep up with me, but he was an utter failure at the party scene. But God had a plan for our lives and orchestrated circumstances to bring that plan to fruition.

My husband was a Reservist and was sent to Korea for a year. During that time, all our friends deserted me. I was looking forward to his return, so we could resume our old life, which we did.

Since I had made no efforts to change, I had to walk around the same mountain again. Six years later, my husband's unit was called to serve in Germany for another full year. I knew from the past what would happen, so I took up with all my unmarried and divorced friends. We partied hearty, and I decided I wanted my freedom to pursue my fulfilled-life unhindered. I forgot my religion.

When my husband returned from Germany, I asked him for a divorce. He was devastated and turned to drink. He became mean and surly. When I was told he had a gun, I felt terrified—too terrified to even consider a divorce. My greatest fear was that if I continued to pursue the divorce, he would try to kill me and the children. I lived in torment for more than three years, never knowing what I was coming home to at night, or if he would come to my workplace and try to kill me there.

In spite of the turmoil in our lives at that time, we continued attending church for the sake of the children. One Sunday, a situation arose that caused us to be in a church not of our faith. When I entered the sanctuary of that church, the power of the Holy Spirit hit me and went through my entire being. I ran to the front pew and cried through the entire service. Afterwards, I went to the altar and prayed the sinner's prayer.

Nothing seemed to change; however, when I went to work the next day, I began to hear voices. One told me, *The prayer you prayed meant nothing; go ahead and get the divorce.* Immediately, another voice spoke and said, *He was calling you for the last time; he will not call again.* This continued all day Monday.

Tuesday began the same way, but at ten in the morning, as I sat at my desk, the power of the Holy Spirit once again went through my body like a lightning bolt.

Then Jesus said, *I have fought Satan for your soul for three days, and I have won. You will never live as you did in the past. Your husband will forgive you, for if he doesn't, his sin will be greater than yours, because I have forgiven you.*

I had a Damascus Road experience. I knew beyond a doubt I had had an encounter with Jesus, and I would never be the same. My life was immediately transformed. Old things passed away, and all things became new. I walked away from my past, my former church, my siblings, and my friends. I never looked back.

I have never regretted my decision. Jesus restored relationships, and I had the privilege of witnessing to my old friends and many of them accepted Jesus. He also gave me a whole host of new friends. I can truthfully say with Jesus, my life is totally fulfilled.

My husband did indeed forgive me, and he gave his heart to Jesus a few days after I did. We still have little in common but Jesus, and that is more than enough. We have learned to accept and respect each other's differences, and because of that, our love for each other continues to grow. We have now been married sixty-four years. No one thought the marriage would last, but with God, all things are possible.

ABOUT THE AUTHOR

Sylvia Hensel writes for two online magazines and has written a Christian devotional and a book for children. Her hope is that God will bless all who read this book.

To see more of this author's work, go to http://faithwriters.com/testimonies2.php.

RISING FROM THE ASHES, A QUEST OF REDEMPTION
By Robert S. Totman

Sitting at the RADARscope in New York on September 11, 2001, I realized for the first time in my life that I *really* had no control over anything. As an air traffic controller, I was adept at managing people, personalities, and very intense air space conflicts; that is, until 9/11. Suddenly, after years of smugness and bragging about working for the FAA, my six-figure income and government job meant nothing to me. I now saw that my job title offered no security whatsoever. In fact, the very place where I sat was a high-value target for a terror strike. Within minutes, a SWAT team arrived, a few men with fancy guns whom we hoped would protect us from hijacked, speeding jumbo jets. I realized how ridiculous this so-called hope was.

I pushed the fear aside and performed my duties, according to my training. Granted, we'd never encountered this particular type of crisis, but I had learned over the years how to keep my cool, regardless of the circumstance, in order to provide a safe, orderly, and expeditious flow of air traffic. And so, miraculously, I did. Surely, God intervened in America's aviation industry that day or there would have been *more* casualties via mid-air collisions, runway incursions, or a myriad of other horrific possibilities.

My shift at the New York Air Route Traffic Control Center ended and I headed home to eastern Long Island. Susan, my wife, had already collected our three-year-old daughter, Beth, from preschool and was waiting for me with our one-year-old son, Robby. We mourned deeply for the day's tragic events and then bedded down in safety, or so we presumed . . .

That's when the terror for *our* family began. At 4 AM on September 12, I sprung out of bed with a huge gasp after waking from a vivid nightmare, in which I had been beneath the rubble of the Twin Towers. It was so clear that it seemed as though waking from the dream literally saved my life. It marked the beginning of two full years of terrible nightmares. Night after night, I must have experienced every imaginable form of death. Each time I woke, I was being snatched from the Grim Reaper. They were so very real that they began controlling my daytime behaviors.

I turned to alcohol and a wide variety of legal and illegal drugs to escape the torment. None of these false comforts could insulate me from the dreadful sting of death, and by the summer of 2002, they cost me my job. The FAA fired me for substance abuse. My security, which was so dear to me, proved unimaginably fragile and fleeting in light of 9/11.

By autumn of 2003, my wife and I were merely occupying the same house, not sharing life together. We had divorce paperwork signed, sealed, and paid for. I feared for my children; if they remained close to me, they could die in a drunken-driving accident or be harmed by my desolate state. Suicide seemed the only answer. Just like the World Trade Center, my facade of security had come crashing down, and my life lay in a heap of ruins.

My wife and I had attended church sporadically over the years and believed we were destined for Heaven. Before I killed myself, I needed to talk to God to seal the deal and tell Him that I couldn't go on any longer—that I was done. *It seems I've placed any and everything before You. I don't really want to kill myself, God, considering the pain it would cause my family, but I don't see any other way. They'll only be hurt more by my presence. This would be best for everyone involved. If there is anything You can do, Jesus, please, intervene.* I began planning my own demise, looking for the right time to execute myself.

A few days later, our family went to church. As soon as we set foot in the sanctuary, I thought I smelled flowers. I asked my wife, "Do you smell that wonderful scent?"

She replied that she did not smell anything; there were no flowers or incense. It was not perfume. The Word of God penetrated my heart like never before. Instantly, the knowledge of Christ became a sweet-smelling aroma to me. Simultaneously, my broken life, wholly given over to God, became a pleasing fragrance to Him (2 Corinthians 2:14-16). I gave my life to God and He intervened to possess it, making an immediate difference.

Instead of horrific nightmares, my dreams were filled with Scripture and Biblical principles. These dreams were so very real that they began reforming my daytime behaviors. All the addictions, the drugs, the alcohol, exasperated by the nightmares, all vanished. I began consuming God's Word day and night, always hungry for more. I would rise throughout the night to inhale the now breathing words of the Bible or fall on my knees to praise God for the extremely dramatic changes I was experiencing. I could hear worship music constantly, never-ending praise to God resounded throughout my entire being (Isaiah 12:2). But, like the absence of explanation for the sweet smell in church that day, apart from God's Word, there was no music physically playing near me. I had passed from one realm of life to another, from a strictly natural and miserable existence filled with pain and suffering, beyond what I knew to be possible, to seeing, tasting, smelling, hearing and feeling blissful, unspeakable things that were being heaped upon me from out of eternity.

My intervening God pursued and overcame my wife within just ten days. No suicide, no divorce; instead, the healing power of God flooded our family. Exactly nine months from the day that she met Jesus, we had a new baby, who we named Grace, delivered by Dr. Christian on a Sunday at the Baptist Hospital. Everything about our lives began proclaiming that Jesus Christ is God. He has since given us yet another magnificent child, Caleb, for a total of four.

In early 2005, I woke one morning and heard my Shepherd's voice, "Put the weight of your world upon My shoulders and I will put My weight upon your world."

As part of my response to heaving all of my weight upon His shoulders, I quit my new job–our only source of income–we sold our home and gave all of our possessions away to benefit the poor. We've been expecting and experiencing His weighty, abundant provision ever since.

These many years later, we still do not go around raising support, nor do I have a job in the traditional sense of the word. I went from giving my all to a fallible and often disintegrating government to being upheld in the infallible and ever-expanding Kingdom of God. My job was an illusion of control and safety; my mission, however, reveals God's control and its security. The King is in control of everything and my life is held out, by Him, to shine like stars in the universe as I hold on to the Word of Life.

ABOUT THE AUTHOR

Robert S. Totman and his wife, Susan, are missionary, church-planting pastors in North Dakota and gifted speakers. They prayerfully consider invitations to minister worldwide, responding to God's call to share His Word in His Love.

To see more of this author's work, go to http://faithwriters.com/testimonies2.php

FINDING THE ANSWER
By Kevin Ingram

When I was twenty-five, I became a Christian. I had reached a point of total frustration and was tired of the battles. Nothing made sense. My life was a series of failures and was getting worse no matter what I tried.

As a teen, I'd escaped from life's problems through alcohol and drugs. A rather naive fifteen-year-old, I began smoking and drinking regularly mostly with other similarly distressed kids. I loved learning, but hated school. I loved living, but hated the life I had. I craved to be loved, but feared the pain of failure.

Ten years later, after I'd spent four years in the military and five years in a marriage that ultimately failed, I had two daughters. I loved them, but they were caught in the trap of divorce. By this time, I had added prescription drugs to my escape plan, and I was using valium and alcohol daily.

My mother and her church prayed earnestly for my salvation. Over the years, God brought people into my life to tell me about him.

In the fall of 1982, I had a girlfriend, who told me her parents were going to make her go to church with them, and that I was going with her, too. I didn't think much about it. I figured I could sleep through a few church services with her. No big deal.

When we got into church, I was shocked. This place was different. The pastor preached with passion and ambition. He smiled a lot and delivered a message of hope and love. People were praising God, speaking in tongues, and shouting. One even hopped up and down praising the Lord. I freaked. I had never seen anything like this before, but it touched me deeply.

My friend showed me where the Bible taught about these things, and I knew I needed to find out more. These people were either crazed or something genuine and supernatural was happening to them. I wanted to know, and I decided to start coming every service to find out.

For several months, I did just that: I came to every service. Sunday morning. Sunday night. Wednesday night. I didn't own a Bible, but Pastor's wife loaned me one until I got one of my own. I read, listened, and learned. If what they believed was true, I wanted to know more about it.

The best part was how the people accepted and encouraged me. They didn't know me well, but were friendly. They lived in a world foreign to me, but they accepted me openly. When I struggled and felt weak or afraid, they loved me sincerely and prayed for me. They didn't just speak about beliefs; they displayed their faith in ways I had never seen. They became the most astounding people in my life.

But even with all the teaching, prayers, and acceptance, I was still lost. I never allowed myself to drink before church, but as soon as it was over, I headed straight for the bar or home and quickly consumed enough numbing substance to escape the world again. Week after week, I attended and learned, and then I headed off to the dead old world of drinking and drugs.

One night in March, I had a fight with my girlfriend. She took off, and I sat through the night getting drunker and more distressed, hating my life more every minute. Sometime after midnight, around 3 AM, I decided it was time for a change, and this time I knew I needed something different. The life

I had been living was never going to work. Drinking and drugs, sex and money, partying and thrills all produced the same results. I was empty, scared, and frustrated. Nothing the world had to offer could ever meet my needs, so I decided to try something else.

I stumbled down the street to the church parsonage and knocked on the door until Pastor and his wife opened up. I told them I had listened to them preach about the good life—a new life—and if it was real, I wanted it now. Once again, they accepted me as I was, sat me down at their kitchen table, and fed me hot chocolate and the Word of God.

I don't remember much of what we said or prayed, but when I left, I knew one thing: I was different! As I walked home in the early predawn darkness, I remember raising one hand to the Lord and saying, "Thank You." I felt so good.

That was over thirty years ago, Friday, March 11, 1983, and early Saturday, March 12. I awoke the next morning a new man, changed and empowered like never before. I could actually feel God's presence in my heart. What a magnificent moment, realizing I had been changed, made new, born again. There is no feeling like it in the world.

I started house cleaning, inside and out. I opened all the booze I owned and poured it down the drain, and I never drank again. I found the thought of drinking alcohol repulsive. I believe it would have made me ill to try. I opened all my medications and flushed them down the toilet, and I never needed them again. *Glory to God*.

I changed everything in my life—from my music to my friends, and I have never regretted one step along the way. It all has been so good. In short, life in Christ has been miraculous. I have had the privilege of preaching, teaching, singing, and pastoring since a few weeks after I was saved, and I have seen many lives changed and souls saved through the years.

I have been blessed with an amazing wife, who has been my best friend for twenty-five years, and a wonderful family.

Everything God touches is blessed, and my life has been touched. It just gets better every day. Through Christ we pray, see miracles, find forgiveness, and by faith find power to overcome the many challenges of life. To God be the Glory. He is Awesome.

ABOUT THE AUTHOR

Kevin Ingram is a pastor, author, evangelist, and musician who currently lives in East Texas with his wife and children. He has more than thirty years of experience in ministry and is currently writing both fiction and non-fiction works, including several novels.

To see more of this author's work, go to http://faithwriters.com/testimonies2.php.

THE LORD'S TERMS
By Sharon Eastman

I was mad at God. I was furious. Who was this grand spiritual entity, who'd grabbed my beautiful mother and took her life so viciously? I was shocked. When the doctor coldly told me that she wouldn't live to see morning, my heart pounded.

I was only twenty-four, and she was forty-seven when she succumbed to a brutal battle with colon cancer. When she'd surrendered her life to Christ two years previously, I humored her. I thought it was a phase. But she grew in beauty and grace like a rosebud blooming into a radiant rose.

Mother had always been a nervous, emotional person as she dealt with a dysfunctional original family and an alcoholic husband. To her friends she was friendly, helpful, and enthusiastic, but to my brothers and me, she was a moody mess.

When she received Christ, peace reigned in her spirit, joy in her soul, and love in her heart. The difference was amazing; her testimony was alive and glowing.

In the meantime, I enjoyed my worldly fun and became estranged from God. Although I attended church as a child, through agnostic teachers and the era of hippie culture, my old-time religious faith faded like my tie-dyed jeans. I dabbled in astrology, leaned towards Eastern religions, and worshipped hard-rock music.

I was an advocate and participant in the free-love movement, which backfired. I caught a minor STD (which I'm thankful healed), and I became pregnant outside of marriage. Fortunately, my boyfriend married me shotgun-wedding style.

Because of my marriage and baby, my life was supposed to flow beautifully. We didn't want to shame and disgrace our families, so I tried to act happy. In reality, I was miserable. We had no money, no good jobs, and no good future.

My only happiness came from loving my darling daughter, Jennifer. I adored her. She was born with yellow jaundice, which turned my soaring spirits into despair. Again, although I wouldn't acknowledge God, he healed my baby with the physician's care and bilirubin lights. After three days of treatment, we brought her home, and we were so happy. When I laid her in her crib for the first time, I cried like the baby she was; I was overwhelmed with the responsibility this new life would entail.

After years of teenage sparring and then being on my own, Mother and I became friends. Grandma loved and spoiled Jennifer. We had many telephone conversations and visits, and she'd often slip me some money to spend on myself. She gave me child-rearing advice, cooking, and household tips. Our relationship healed from the devastation my out-of-wedlock pregnancy wrought.

Although it has been almost forty years since Mother's death, a ringing phone brings thoughts of her. Death slapped me in the face. I awoke to its reality as I had lost the most precious diamond in my life. I searched the Scriptures with vigor. I prayed sincerely and intently seeking Jesus, this God, the author of life and death.

Fortunately, Sue—a wonderful Christian woman—invited me to her neighborhood Bible study. I said a meek, "Yes," but went eagerly.

On a weekly basis, about seven women met at her home, where we shared delicious food for the body and soul. We

The Lord's Terms

came from all faiths and all kinds of lives, but we had two things in common: we liked to talk, and we ached for God. Some of Sue's church friends and missionaries also attended.

I enjoyed the Bible-study lessons, and I was enthralled with the fellowship. I felt comfortable, peaceful, and loved. Prayer request time was my favorite. I solemnly listened to the requests and was astonished by God's answers. Sometimes he said, "Yes," and sometimes he said, "No," but he always answered.

I still grieved for my mother, but in a three-year period, some of my dreams came true. My husband was flourishing at work; Jennifer was healthy and growing; I had my own home; and best of all, I had a newborn baby boy, Michael.

Despite my good fortune, I still felt as if the God-spot in my heart was empty. It took three, long, stubborn years until I believed God's Word was true, and I needed the Savior, Jesus Christ. Besides, I wanted what my Bible-study friends had: peace, love, joy, and Christian fellowship.

One day, shortly after Michael's birth, I asked Sue to lead me to the Lord. I sought salvation on the Lord's terms. She dropped everything and came to my side. We prayed, and I surrendered my life to God. I believed fervently Jesus was the Way, the Truth, and the Life; I believed no one comes to the Father but by Jesus (John 14:6 KJV).

Sue suggested I write the date in my Bible. Upon leaving she said, "Look at your life next year, and see how it has changed."

Three days after I prayed this prayer, I gradually awoke in a mental hospital. I had suffered a post partum psychosis. I didn't know who I was, where I was, or what I was. Slowly, the miracle medications of the late '70s took effect, and six dreary weeks later, I was released. Although I was dazed and confused, I never lost my faith in Christ. I prayed for my family and the other patients. I sang the hymns of my childhood because I didn't know Scriptures. The Lord really blessed and upheld me during this trying time.

Life continued as always, and I started attending church. I made new friends and learned more about the Scriptures and God. I worshipped him with all my heart. But I was haunted by this psychotic experience, and I pleaded for the Lord to deliver me from this affliction and not to let it happen again.

To my dismay, I had episode upon episode for the next ten years. Finally, during my last hospitalization, they diagnosed my malady as schizoaffective disorder—a mental illness, with some features of schizophrenia and some of a mood disorder. The problems may be alleviated by medications (in my case, faith and prayer, too).

This affliction is my "thorn in the flesh." I'll have to cope with it all my life. With the exception of a few weak periods or moments, I am high functioning. I maintain a household and care for my family and my ninety-two-year-old father. I also write Christian poetry and prose.

I praise the Lord for this disorder. Because of it, I depend on him for everything. I especially heed the Scripture, *"For God hath not given us the spirit of fear, but of power, and of love, and of a sound mind" (2 Timothy 1:7 KJV).*

I enjoy my blessed life, but I can't wait to see Jesus face-to-face in glory some day. I'll forget my earthly illness and just praise and worship him forever!

ABOUT THE AUTHOR

Sharon Eastman is a grandmother of two young children and mother of a super daughter and son. She writes Christian poetry and prose. This testimony is true after serving over thirty years for the Lord and was written with all the love in her heart for the Lord.

To see more of this author's work, go to http://faithwriters.com/testimonies2.php.

HE HEARD MY PRAYER!
By Luella Campbell

Morning by morning, I knelt beside my hotel-room bed with tears streaming down my cheeks, uttering the same prayer because I knew no other. *"Our Father, who art in Heaven, hallowed be thy name..." (Matthew 6:9 KJV)*

I longed to know; who was I? All I knew was that I was a lonely teenager who instinctively felt that something was missing, but did not know what it was or where to find it. My mother said I should have been a boy; she favoured my brother and hounded me to be productive and to do so-called girl things like sewing, knitting, cooking, and baking. But I liked to read... I often hid under the bed or in the toilet with a book until Mother called me. My father was kindly, but rather distant and busy at what he did best–running a business. My brother and his friends treated me with disdain. After all, I was just his kid sister.

I was brought up in an average middle-class family; I had one sibling, an older brother, and parents who faithfully ensured that we all attended church. Outwardly, I was a model child at home, at school, a model student; I shone in academic studies, but not in sports. Being seen as a brainy kid did not make me very popular, especially among the sporty types. I was shy and introverted, had few friends, and kept to myself.

I attended Sunday school with my big brother from the age of eighteen months–I was so small that my chubby legs were too short to reach the floor when I sat on my toddler-sized chair. There I learnt to parrot the Lord's Prayer. I also learnt many other things in Sunday school during my growing-up years. Scripture verses were like a second language to me; Scripture examinations every year, from the time I could read and write, saw to that.

As I moved into my teenage years, loneliness descended on me like a dark cloud. It ate at my insides and nothing seemed to quench my thirst for whatever was missing, not even the times I spent with a few young girls whom I called friends.

I have not yet explained how I came to be kneeling in a hotel room. My parents were building a new home and, for the three months it took to complete the house, we had to make do with hotel accommodation. My bedroom was at the rear of the hotel, a small, stark room with a cupboard, a dressing table, and an iron bedstead against the wall, facing the parking area. It had one feature I loved–the early morning sun streaming in through the window, which warmed my back as I knelt and prayed.

I may have parroted my hotel-room prayer, but my heart was full of yearning–and the Father heard my cry. I did not know it then, but there was a plan unfolding that would sweep me into a new life I could never have imagined possible.

A few months later on April 1, 1956, with the gentle invitation of an old hymn, "Softly and Tenderly," by Will L. Thompson, ringing in my ears, I knelt on the dusty ground in a marquee tent on the banks of the Igoda River, and prayed a different prayer. *Father, thank you for sending Jesus to be my Saviour.* All the pain of loneliness and the dark cloud that had hung over me for many months, lifted. A presence had come in to abide with me, forever. It was Easter Sunday, and a day I would never forget. A group of young people from churches in the Border area of the Eastern Cape, South Africa, gathered for the first time for a combined Easter Camp on a farm on the Igoda River. The camp speaker for the weekend was Lauritz Larsen, a diminutive Nordic preacher. His stature may have been small, but his heart was big–and his message even bigger. He presented Jesus in a way I had never considered before, in spite of years of teaching in Sunday school. For the first time, the eyes of this teenage girl were opened to the beauty of the "Friend of sinners."

With tears flowing once more, I knelt in the dust and opened my heart to the Prince of Peace. At that moment, I may not have understood everything, but one thing I knew–I would never be lonely again. There was One who had come to live inside me, who would never leave me, and never fail me.

Fifty-eight years have come and gone since that day when my life changed forever. No drama, no fireworks, or neon lights marked the occasion, but on that day, my name was recorded in the Lamb's Book of Life.

Since then, I have had fifty-eight years of living, failing, then getting up and going on, but most of all, learning to know and love my Prince. In that time, I have lived through personal struggles, a failed marriage, soured friendships, the pain of betrayal, as well as raising four sons, and walking with them through their personal struggles. Now, I have the calm waters of joy and fulfilment, dreams realised and new dreams coming alive. Together, they have made up the hotchpotch of my life in a fallen world, all thrown together to create the environment in which the unparalleled beauty of my Saviour and Friend is being revealed.

He heard my prayer!

ABOUT THE AUTHOR

Luella Campbell is a retired nurse, mother, and grandmother. As pastoral assistant at her church in South Africa, she teaches discipleship classes, writes teaching materials, articles for her church magazine, and daily blogs.

To see more of this author's work, go to http://faithwriters.com/testimonies2.php

ACCOUCHEMENT
By Cindy Maness

*B**e still. You can do this. It will be a great release. No more pain. No more guilt. No more shame. But…"Thou shall not kill."* Dollops of tears plopped onto the blade as it convulsed over my wrist.

My mind zoomed back in time like a roller coaster plunging down its course. Words like fangs bit into my flesh; more words felt like talons raping me. If *Hate* is a destroyer, *Indifference* is her heinous cousin who invests nothing into nothing. *Will it ever end?* I almost terminated this farce of a life once before. *Let me leave the world being successful with at least one thing.* Like a scar, I could see one word, *unlovable*, written on my battered heart.

Again, my brain relived a barrage of moments and a dowry of smoldering dreams. Rejection, abuse, homelessness, drugs, alcohol, rape, suicide, depression, demons, and rage were some of my tormenters. However, the commander's name of that band of thieves was *Murder*.

I don't remember the name of the place; all I know is that I went there filled with fear. The clinic was located on one of the top floors in an unremarkable building. Its windows glared down at the grimy part of the city. Old, rumpled magazines were strewn on hand-me-down tables. Crashing into the walls of my insides were silent screams, desperately searching for release. *This cannot be right!* Panic crawled through my pores. *Help me! Does anyone care what's about to happen? I wish someone would stop this. I wish I could stop this! It's just a blob of tissue. I have to do it or my parents will send me away. I'm so confused.*

I was sixteen years old when a nurse ushered me into the loneliest room in the world. After discarding my clothes, I waited in my nakedness for her to hand me a thin, backless gown that hundreds had worn before me, and I noticed the room felt chilly, effete, and gray. As I climbed onto the steel table, I glimpsed a smear of my reflection that I barely recognized.

Suddenly, I had a difficult time reigning in my frenzied emotions. My heart thrashed, my adrenalin spiked, and I desperately wanted to hold on to something familiar. When the nurse and doctor came in, the nurse said, "There's nothing to worry about. Everything will be over soon."

I felt so nervous, and they really didn't explain what they were going to do; they just had me put my feet in the stirrups and turned on a machine. It was like a little vacuum cleaner that had a suction hose on the end of it. They used it to suck out my baby, the baby that God had created inside of me. My baby, whose eyes I would never see, whose smile I would never know, whose laughter I would never hear, whose hugs I would never feel, disappeared into the wretched machine. When they put the hose inside of me, not only did it end all of my child's hopes and dreams for this life, it also ended a whole lineage of future generations for that child, including parties, laughter, graduations, weddings, and birth announcements. Everything was gone in one irretrievable moment. They sucked my baby out of me while I clenched a stranger's hand the entire time. Then, they began to scrape the remains from my womb, as to make sure they finished the job.

I remember the nurses and doctors were smiling. During the worst moment of my life, they were smiling. I couldn't believe it and thought, *Oh, come on, everybody; let's all sing,*

"If you're happy and you know it clap your hands..." My baby's hands would never clap. They were gone. I felt like I was about to go insane.

Left with a deflated void, all I could think about was escaping that place after it had swallowed me. *How will I ever get over assassinating my own child; how does any mother?*

My parents and I never spoke of it again. I thought it only right to give my baby a name. I decided on Jaime.

My mind collapsed back into the present. I stared at the blade hovering over my wrist. Suddenly, I became aware of a man's voice coming from the TV. "It doesn't matter where you've been. It doesn't matter what you've done. God loves you *so* much that He sent His son to die for you."

I heard those words, and the embryo of truth was born. *Could it be true?* I latched onto that seed of hope with everything in me, and I dropped to my knees. The dam burst and I wept rivers as I begged God to come into my life.

Then, two amazing things happened. First, I heard a voice. "Be still, my beloved child, and know that I am God." Next, wave after wave of a love, which I had always been a stranger to, engulfed me. It was a powerful, electrifying, surge of God's healing, unadulterated love. He forgave all of my transgressions.

For the next thirty-two years, God accompanied me on an untamed journey of my rebirth. God graciously exposed and sorted the lies from the truth. The God I know today looks very different from the one I worshiped before I encountered His love on that day.

I learned that God *is* love. He is real and is the source of all goodness. I am a part of the greatest love story ever written, and He was intentional when He created me. Giving up everything, He died on a cross in order to bring meaning and purpose to my life. My life has not been perfect, and I still experience times of trials; yet, the thing I remember during those times is that the God of the universe loves me fiercely and I am never alone.

I know that Jaime went straight into my Father's arms that day. She is waiting for me, and I can't wait to meet her and have her meet my other eight children and nine grandchildren. I have watched in wonder as God restored me, and I am ripe with hope. He didn't allow my horrible experiences to be wasted; instead, he took my seemingly hopeless situation, redeemed it, and transformed me with His brilliance so that I now shine. Without a doubt, I know how much He loves me and all of His children.

I love how Jesus, who is light and knows where darkness lives, took me by the hand and led me home to His heart. He saw me not as I was but who I was to become. He values me and all life.

Recently, I looked up the meaning of Jaime's name. In French, *J'aime*, means, "I love."

ABOUT THE AUTHOR

Originally, from Wisconsin, Cindy Maness now lives in Virginia with her husband. She loves talking about Jesus, reading, writing and playing with her grandchildren who continually find creative ways to bring wonder and laughter to her life.

To see more of this author's work, go to http://faithwriters.com/testimonies2.php

FIVE YEARS WITHOUT FEAR
By Lynn Gipson

What a difference five years can make. In that period, I became a new person with Jesus Christ as my Lord and Savior. In those few years, I became fearless.

Five years ago, I was dying. The prior six months had been one long death sentence for me. Although I had been through several surgeries for brain and stage-four colon cancer, my prognosis was not good. I was not expected to live long.

Those six months were life changing for me. The days following my emergency surgery to have a brain tumor removed were a real wake-up call. That is when God came to me in the middle of the night and rained such grace down upon me; sometimes I still find it all so hard to believe.

Three months later, following the brain surgery, a colostomy, hysterectomy, and having my gall bladder removed, He appeared to me every night in that cold, stark, hospital room. Surrounding me with His omnipotent power, He healed my body, comforted my spirit, and saved my soul from eternal damnation.

Before that time in my life, I had only prayed to an unknown God. I believed there was a higher power, but never really understood the meaning of faith. I had lived in fear most of my life, having come from a family that thrived on fear. I prayed constantly, but I still felt afraid. That is because, until my life was literally in God's hands, I did not know exactly what faith was. I was fifty-eight years old before I truly came to know who Christ was, and that miracles really do happen.

Those lonely days and nights of a month-long hospital stay taught me how to have faith. The most amazing thing about it all was that I didn't have to go looking for it. Faith came to me! Jesus Christ stood before me and filled me with the love, hope, and forgiveness I had been searching for all of my life. I would wake up in the middle of the night and feel His Spirit all around me. It was a presence of warmth and love, and somehow I knew it to be that of Jesus.

In the five years since my final major surgery, I have been through chemotherapy, radiation, and laser ablations. Throughout it all, I have never once been afraid. Fear was once my constant companion, but no more. I came to realize that with faith, all things are possible, and with my Lord and Savior by my side, I have absolutely nothing to be afraid of.

When I let go and let God have total and complete control, miracles abounded. He took care of my financial problems, saw that health insurance was granted, and, lo and behold, my cancer was healed. For two years, my body was in remission.

Then, a year and a half ago, a small tumor in some scar tissue reared its ugly head. But once again, God spoke. On my last doctor's visit, He blessed me with yet another miracle. My doctor informed me that he thought the tumor was dead. Just another way God reassures me that He, and He alone, is in control.

Yes, Jesus saved my life five years ago, but my life was worth nothing until I came to know Him. One might think I am most grateful to Him for allowing me to live these last few years, but I am even more grateful to Him for saving my soul. Knowing my soul is in Christ makes me unafraid of life and even death.

Another amazing thing has happened to me in the last five years. God put upon my heart the desire to become a writer in order to tell others what a Christ-filled life can do. I never thought I could write, but God told me I could. And so I do. I write about my experiences to let others know that with God there is nothing to fear.

Realizing my life belongs to Christ gives me a peace and fearlessness I have craved and longed for all my life. Whatever happens in the next five years, whether it be on earth or in Heaven, I will fear no evil, for He is with me.

ABOUT THE AUTHOR

Lynn Gipson is a cancer survivor who is battling again. In addition to being a dedicated mom and proud grandmother, she is an author and contributes to various online magazines.

To see more of this author's work, go to http://faithwriters.com/testimonies2.php

NEW HOPE AND PURPOSE
By Maria Lee

When I was sixteen, I changed my routine by retreating into the empty dining room. Instead of doing my homework, I poured my thoughts out on paper. After contemplating my notes, I decided to write a suicide letter.

Growing up, my world centered on my family, which consisted of my parents, five sisters, four brothers, and me, the third-born. My mother worked tediously raising ten children, and my father worked industriously at his business providing for his large family. Both parents were perfectionists and expected their children to achieve academically and live uprightly. They scolded me severely when I didn't achieve their level of success.

I felt ashamed that I could not fulfill my parents' expectations and felt inferior compared to my siblings. Consequently, my self-worth diminished; I withdrew into a shell of emotional knots of confusion and loneliness, and I felt disconnected from my family.

Depression led to darkness, which eventually overshadowed me. As I sat alone in the dining room, considering how to kill myself, God had other plans for me and intervened on my behalf. Before I could follow through with my intentions, my sister entered the room and sat next to me to do her homework. Looking at her face made me realize that I had to keep trying.

When I failed high school, my world crumpled once more as horrible thoughts kept replaying in my mind. *I'm not good enough. Nobody likes me. I'm a failure.* Self-rejection took root in my heart, and I wanted to die. Feeling desperate, I even consulted an occult, tealeaf reader for help and guidance.

Things seemed better for a while. I finished high school and even went on to graduate from secretarial college. At my first job, I met Sterling Lee. Before long, a romance blossomed, and we became husband and wife in 1971. Initially, Sterling was attentive to my needs and romantic. *My life's perfect now,* I thought.

In just four short years, we had two children, Gordon and Stacey, and moved to Toronto, Canada, hours away from my family and friends. Because Sterling worked excessively, loneliness crept in. I felt abandoned and unloved, stuck at home with two small children, and no family or friends.

In an attempt to ward off my feelings, I took the children to the park on a beautiful day where I saw a little girl singing, "Jesus Loves Me," by Anna Bartlett Warner and William Batchelder Bradbury. The words of the song penetrated my soul. "Jesus loves me–this I know, For the Bible tells me so..." As I listened to her, tears welled up in my eyes. I believe God led me to the park and sent a messenger in the form of a little girl to affirm to me that Jesus, indeed, loves me.

A year after I had Stacey, I decided to try to pursue my passion in floristry. I desperately needed to feel fulfilled and to spend time with adults. Unfortunately, I only lasted a week before my postpartum depression crashed through and flattened my dream.

On my last day of work, my co-worker, Evelyn, tried to console me. She and her boyfriend drove me to the bus stop, and she handed me a beautiful white Bible. She prayed and embraced me; we parted, and I never saw her again. I believe that God directed Evelyn to give me my first Bible. I started reading the words that would eventually satisfy my hunger for God and change my life forever.

Before I completed my transformation, I expected Sterling to understand my feelings, but he seemed clueless. He focused on providing for his family. Instead of communicating with him, I harbored resentment and anger. Occasionally, my frustration spewed onto our children; consequently, I hated myself more. Something had to change.

Several years later, I listened to the testimony of an ex-prostitute whose life changed when she surrendered her life to Jesus. Immediately, the Holy Spirit convicted me of my sins. With my whole heart and faith, I sobbed as I prayed with the host of the show. *Dear Jesus, please forgive me of my sins and come into my heart. I need you to be my Lord and Savior. In your precious name, I pray. Amen.* It took several minutes for me to stop crying and gather my thoughts. Suddenly, the power of God came upon me and transformed my heart; I felt God's love and peace flowing in me.

When Sterling arrived home, I felt a new love for him. I shared my experience and asked, "Would you like to say the same prayer and give your life to Jesus, too?"

He answered, "Yes," and then we hugged each other and cried as we prayed. God performed a miracle in our hearts, and from that night on, our lives gradually changed. Neither of us totally understood, but by faith, we prayed, placing our trust in Jesus. That night marked the beginning of Sterling, our children, and me growing together in the Lord.

When we told our families and friends of our faith, we gave all praise and glory to God for all He did in us. Our new life as Christians had begun.

> *"And they have conquered him by the blood of the Lamb and by the word of their testimony, for they loved not their lives even unto death" (Revelation 12:11 NASB)*

New Hope and Purpose

Sterling and I received the baptism of the Holy Spirit with the evidence of speaking in tongues on separate occasions. The Lordship of Jesus became prominent in my life and my self-centeredness became less as I began renewing my mind with the Scriptures. Love and forgiveness were the first lesson God taught me. I began to see myself from God's perspective. Knowing He has a plan, a purpose, hope, and a future for my life gave me peace and security, even when my husband had to work overtime.

About six weeks later, I experienced excruciating headaches, nightmares, and strange voices spoke though my own voice. This phenomenon caused us to discern a demonic attack. Being a new Christian, I was ignorant of spiritual warfare, ignorant of who God is and His power, and illiterate of the Scriptures. Yet, God, in His love, and grace, taught Sterling what to do. When I started screaming and shaking, he started praying for me.

He would sit up quickly and hold me in his arms and say, "In the name of Jesus, devil, leave my wife now." On one occasion, at the sound of, *Jesus,* I heard a roar like a lion.

I contacted a Christian ministry, and a group of three people came to our home. They prayed for my deliverance, and I renounced all occult involvement in my life. I told them I had a vision of a crystal castle, and they told me it was the New Jerusalem as recorded in Revelation 21. That night, as I read the Scripture, my faith was strengthened, knowing that God chose to reveal this passage of the New Jerusalem, a place called Heaven reserved for all who believe in Jesus.

I praise and thank the Lord for effectually changing my life and my husband's. I have God's peace and assurance that my purpose is to live and reign with Jesus eternally and to tell the world about the wonderful grace of God.

> *"He said to them, 'Go into all the world and preach the gospel to all creation.'" (Mark 16:15 NIV)*

ABOUT THE AUTHOR

Maria A. Lee, author of the gospel tract, "Timeless Truths about Your Destiny," lives in Miami, Florida, with her husband, Sterling. Maria is a student at Alpha and Omega Bible Institute. She uses her gifts as a florist, artist, and writer to inspire love, joy, faith, and hope in people's lives.

To see more of this author's work, go to http://faithwriters.com/testimonies2.php.

GOD'S POWERFUL SAVING WORK IN MY LIFE
By Ken Grant

I sat in the small room with Victor, the star guard for the varsity basketball team and a senior. I was a sophomore who couldn't make the junior varsity team. We seemingly had little in common. Yet, God brought us together for a specific purpose. God had been pursuing me for some time, but now Victor was the final instrument in drawing me in. Jesus promised his disciples that he would make them fishers of men, and Victor was truly a fisher of men. He drew me to God in that small room and my life changed forever.

I was the child of a believing mother and an unbelieving father. To this day, I don't understand why my mother rejected the council of the Lord and married a man who was unwilling to trust in Christ for salvation. I loved my father to the day that he died, but he consistently rejected the way of faith to his own destruction. My mother took me to church when I was young. She tried to introduce me to the way of faith, but sadly, the church that she was a part of was focused on tradition rather than faith. I never met Jesus in that church, and so, over time, my father's unbelief and worldly ways began to draw me away.

One day I made a clear break from the way of faith. I told my mother, "I don't want to go to church anymore."

My mother showed loved, but today, I realize that I hurt her by rejecting her faith and choosing to live the way of pleasing the flesh. On Sunday, rather than go to church, I slept in and watched whatever sport was in season. I followed my father's example of pleasing the flesh. Because my parents had me later in their lives, I was free to do whatever I wanted. I thought it a good life, but it lacked the presence of God. Yet, God did not leave me. Although I didn't deserve it, he imprinted me with his presence. In Sunday school, the teachers taught me the Lord's Prayer. For some reason, long after I stopped going to church, I continued to pray that prayer every night before going to sleep.

"Our Father who art in heaven, hallowed be thy name. Thy kingdom come. Thy will be done, on earth as it is in heaven. Give us this day our daily bread. And forgive us our trespasses, as we forgive those who trespass against us. And lead us not into temptation, but deliver us from evil. For thine is the kingdom and the power and the glory forever. Amen."
(Matthew 6:9-13 KJV)

I had little understanding of the words, but every night I was speaking the Word of God. God's Word had power even when I didn't understand it fully. Although I had done things my way, God never let me out of His sight. He loved me enough to send his son, Jesus, to die for my sins, and he loved me enough to pursue me when I walked away from him.

As I entered my freshman year of high school, God regularly sent me visions of my death. In my dream, I recall floating in nothingness, aware that I had died, but cognizant that all around me was nothingness. God was giving me a taste, a small taste, of the reality of life without his presence. Questions about God began to fill my mind, but I had no one in my life who could give me answers. I spent that year in frustration and confusion, but happily, God was not done working in my life.

During my sophomore year of high school, I decided to try out for the junior varsity basketball team. I didn't end up making the team, but that decision led to a complete transformation in my life. One day as I was practicing, the head coach of the varsity basketball team came up to me. I have no idea how he knew who I was, but his choice was critical in the course of my life. He asked me, "How would you like to help out on the varsity team, keep the stats, collect the balls at the end of practice, and do a few other things here and there?"

The opportunity to be around varsity basketball players was too good to pass up. "Of course I'll do it. That sounds awesome," I said confidently.

That is how I ended up in the treatment room with Victor. Victor was not only the star of the basketball team, but more importantly, he led the campus Bible study. He was a follower of Jesus Christ, and God led me directly to him to hear the words of life. Victor had injured his ankle, and it was my responsibility to open that small room so that he could ice it. I unlocked the door for Victor and began to leave.

"Come in and sit with me," Victor said.

The opportunity to hang out with a senior star athlete was too good to be true. I sat down and amazingly, he began to speak to me about the love of God, how Jesus sacrificed himself for my sins, and the opportunity to respond in faith to his offer. He answered every question that I had.

Even today, I remember the moment clearly. "Yes, I want to receive Jesus Christ as my savior and Lord."

The God that I had heard spoken of in vague terms had now become real to me. I became a follower of Jesus Christ. God has since used me to declare my faith and disciple others in the way of Christ in many places all over the world. Every day I live is a testimony of God's faithfulness in never giving up on me and of the willingness of my friend, Victor, to share faithfully the good news to me. To this day, Victor is a good friend, but Jesus is my everything. Today, I am a follower of Jesus Christ and will one day live in the presence of God forever.

ABOUT THE AUTHOR

Ken Grant is a fifty-year-old freelance writer from Santa Ana, California. He has been a follower of Jesus Christ for thirty-five years. He has one published novel, *So Great a Salvation*, and contributes material to a number of other on-line publishing sites.

A BRAND NEW HEART
By Elizabeth Gordon

On Christmas morning, 1960, in the southern part of Dallas, a soft, billowy snow covered the ground. As usual, on this special day, everyone scurried around in my grandmother's cozy kitchen preparing the Christmas tamales. I am certain my grandfather sang while playing his guitar or violin. This was one of his joyous expressions, whenever he was happy and energetic, which was most of his life. All too soon, my mother, who was nine months pregnant with me, began to feel uneasy; her water broke, and my story began.

On that beautiful Christmas day, I came into the world after my frail mother endured hours of aches and pains. As she held me in her arms, I imagine that she had no idea what my future held. My mother was already pregnant with me when she met and married my stepfather, and she became a spirit-filled Christian.

Now, I realize how her impartation affected my little spirit to desire the same encounter. At the age of eight, I became a spirit-filled Christian as well.

Even though my mother and stepfather were Christians, they were a dysfunctional couple. They prayed, taught my sister and me the Word, preached the Word, and memorized Scriptures, but they never really conquered pains from their past. In those days, people thought the exposure of an imperfect lifestyle would hurt one's ministry. People didn't talk about what happened behind closed doors. It was easier to keep family secrets hidden from outsiders. Not admitting to the shame of it all helped to keep their fears alive. My little world, however, was haunted and traumatized with continual wretched pain that I cannot describe.

I have one sister who experienced more of the brutal abuse. She is eighteen months older than I am. My stepfather adopted her; he didn't raise her from birth as he did with me. I believe this played a role in his favoritism toward me. Even so, our lives were not easy. My parents were missionaries, so we moved around a lot and were homeschooled for most of our lives. At times, we were forbidden to talk, share expressive thoughts, or giggle unless he was in a good mood. He controlled our lives and kept us in fear continually. He would not allow our mother to teach us Spanish, which was our cultural language. He feared that we would tell her how he was abusing us, and another language would not allow him to control us.

If I even insinuated a different view or opinion, he whipped me with boards and belts and locked me in the closet. In front of family members, he would ask, "Do you love me?"

Hanging my head in shame, I refused to answer. That only antagonized him more. He grabbed my arm and yanked me into the bathroom to beat me.

My family detested him and told my mother to leave, but somehow he would convince her that the family was wrong and he was always right. He would say, "The enemy is trying to split us up."

As time went on, the secret abuse of molestation was exposed. After all the tears were shed, my mother prayed and spoke with someone from church. In the end, she decided to forgive him and go back. I was devastated but had no say in the matter. My mother was co-dependent; she needed a man in her life–regardless of the pain he caused my sister and me.

When we were older, they allowed us to attend public school, but my stepfather refused to give us permission to attend any school functions, games, or dances. We couldn't have friends spend the night or go to sleepovers like other girls our age. Our lives were sheltered, and my sister and I had to complete our much-desired education on our own. Without any parental help or encouragement, we held on to one another.

Moreover, we both had to seek help and healing for the little lost girls that were locked in a dungeon of horror. When I became an adult, I had agonizing dreams of being buried alive. This was due to my fears that were trapped in my soul.

My personal healing was overwhelmingly blissful. About twenty years ago, I joined a class at church in order to bring closure to my traumatic past. The third class was on shame. As I sat there, I listened to the facilitator explain about shame and the effect it has on humanity. The Holy Spirit spoke to me and said, "You are shame-based; you're ashamed of who you are, what has been done to you, what you've done, and what you've become or haven't become."

It felt like someone splashed a cold glass of water on my face. I couldn't get home fast enough. I ran in my room, locked my door, grabbed a Kleenex box, put a CD on, and fell to my knees. I began to sob. My heart was ready, and my soul needed God.

Once I gathered my composure, I talked to God. *Dear Jesus, oh I need you so much right now. Please help me. I feel like I've fallen into a pit of despair. I feel alone and full of hate. Somehow, I've turned into this mean, ugly, obnoxious person. I'm no better than my stepfather is, and I hate him. I don't want to be like him any more, not for one more second! Please, God, help me change. I know I need forgiveness, and I'm not strong enough to forgive those who have hurt me. But if You will forgive me, I know you can help me to let go of everything.*

Instantly, I felt a tremendous weight fall off my back. The lift was so physically manifested that I knew someone was there in the room with me. Instantly, I collapsed, face down, and began to sob uncontrollably because, at that very moment, God became my Father.

When I gathered my stamina, I slowly arose in a marvelously divine ecstasy. My whole body had been affected by a love I had never experienced. My mind, heart, and spirit were new. I felt so light and speechless. Words have never been able to describe that heavenly moment. God completely erased my pain, and I became a person full of Father's love.

ABOUT THE AUTHOR

Elizabeth Gordon has been a Christian since the age of eight. She is an author and is dedicated to her family. She and her husband currently reside in the San Antonio, Texas, area. She enjoys art, music, singing, and playing with her dog, Tinkerbelle.

To see more of this author's work, go to http://faithwriters.com/testimonies2.php.

TWO-EDGED SWORD
By Richard McCaw

"Now, Richard," said my mother that Sunday morning, probably with a dishtowel over her shoulder as she stood at the gate, "hold your sister's hand every time you cross the street!" As we hurried down the road along the sidewalk, she may have called after us, "And watch out for cars!"

So I grabbed my sister's hand, and shortly we stood on the sidewalk along Orange Street, watching cars whizz by. We soon reached the gray wooden Assembly Hall of the Brethren Church, and I found myself sitting with the other nine-year-old boys in my Sunday school class. But the teacher sounded like a monotonous drum, beating the same rhythm week after week.

"Who can say our golden text today?" she asked. A few hands went up. She pointed to a boy in the front. He rattled off the verse confidently. Then she said, "Let's all say the verse together!"

Most of us stumbled through the verse. Then, as she started her lecture, a boy raised his hand. The teacher looked at him, "Yes?"

"May I go outside for a drink of water, Miss?"

"Go ahead!" she said. He was out in a flash.

Hmm, I reasoned. *Perhaps I could raise my hand and get outside too.* So I raised my hand and, in no time, I was outside. That was the last time I attended that Sunday school. I had graduated to my own quiet space where I was lord of all I could see, touch, and feel.

Later, when I was about twelve and a half, my mother had been sending us to a different Sunday school, which was held on the lawn of a large house along Constant Spring Road.

Have you ever felt a strong need to be seen and heard, a desire to be well thought of by others? At home, have you ever pushed your siblings about? Or, at work, have you ever shoved your junior employees around, just so that they knew exactly who was in charge? Well, that same desire for self-glory came over me. One day, in a Bible class, I felt that strong urge to pass off a smart remark and get a little attention my way.

We all sat outside on wooden chairs with grass under our feet. Tall coconut trees, leafy mango trees, various garden trees, and low-lying bush were scattered across the wide lawn. Sometimes, I pulled a girl's hair and when she turned around, I rebuked the nearest boy with an innocent look on my face. "Why are you troubling the girl?"

That particular Sunday afternoon, the young lady teaching the class moved Bible characters about from story to story with the visual help of flannelgraph.* With only a desert scene to work with, she illustrated the story by moving a ship carrying Jesus and the disciples on to that same desert scene.

"How come they're driving the ship on dry land?" I shouted, raising my hand. Everyone laughed, and I, the loudest.

At first, I thought I had escaped with that smart remark. However, after the class had been dismissed, she called me aside and began to scold me privately.

"Richard," she began. I hardly looked up at her. "Disturbing others while I'm telling a story is not very nice, is it?" Suddenly, I felt like a cornered mouse, looking to escape her penetrating eyes. Not answering, I kept looking down on the ground. "And I know you think it's funny, but with only a desert scene to tell the story of Moses, when I teach about Jesus and His disciples in the ship, everyone has to imagine sea all around. Why did you ask if the ship was driving on sand in the middle of the desert? Everyone is going to laugh and that distracts the whole class!"

What caused me to be disruptive? A need for attention? A need to be loved? No doubt, a need for the deep, deep love of God: the only thing that could really satisfy my heart.

After that teacher had scolded me, I was tormented and sure that if I had died right then, I would have gone straight to Hell. I was terrified! I remembered my wild reputation with Sunday school teachers, lies I had told, and the stealing of grapes. The Spirit of God was definitely at work convicting me of my sins. Embarrassed, I never returned to that class.

Then, the Sunday night before my thirteenth birthday, my mother took us to Bethany Gospel Hall, a Brethren church on Hagley Park Road, Kingston. People from all over the city had come to hear Harold Wildish, a well-known English evangelist, and the church was crowded. Although ceiling fans were whirring, many were busily fanning. You could hear the shuffling of leaves as many turned the pages of their Bibles. I recall the tall preacher's large, clear face and tiny moustache. As the service ended, he invited anyone who wanted to be saved to come forward.

"You'll receive a free booklet of John's Gospel," he added.

Free booklet! I thought. Since I was a keen reader, I went forward.

Someone warmly greeted me with outstretched hand and told me, "Sit down here, son!"

As I sat down on the front seat, Marion Wildish, the preacher's wife, a short, plump English woman with an elegant church hat, came and sat beside me. Whatever she said must have flown through one ear and out the other. Only one thing remained with me: "Say this after me: I am His and He is mine!"

"I am His and He is mine!" I repeated. Those words struck my spirit like a nail well hammered in. Suddenly, the truth broke forcibly upon me that the God of the universe actually owned me, and I had a special relationship with Him as His very own friend. What a revelation and turning point! I was born again into the Kingdom of God. Thank God for my mother, who did not send me, but took me to church to hear God's Word.

Oh, and remember that Sunday school class from which I had run away? Two years later, at the age of fifteen, I returned to that same Sunday school to teach. In 1963, a local Christian magazine called *The Caribbean Challenge* published my testimony with the title 'I turned my back on God!' Running away from the God of the universe? From personal experience, I can tell you that it does not work!

I had proven for myself that *"the word of God is living and powerful, and sharper than any two-edged sword" (Hebrews 4:12 NKJV)*. It had broken through all the parts of my personality, even my soul and spirit, and must have reached deep into my very joints and marrow. It had searched into my thoughts and my heart's (Hebrews 4:12).

I began to perceive that the God of the universe, who had created me miraculously in my mother's womb, had brought me out of darkness into His marvelous light.

Today, I can say, "He is worthy to receive ceaseless praises!" Like the angels in Heaven, who worship at His throne, and the apostles and elders mentioned in the Revelation, I sometimes come before Him. Raising my hands like the psalmist David did, I sing and worship Him.

Could I have made a better connection? Miracle of miracles, I met the King of the universe and we became special friends!

* N. B. Flannelgraph: a flannel board, resting on an easel.

ABOUT THE AUTHOR

Richard McCaw, a Caribbean writer, has publishing credits of poetry, short stories, one serialized novel, devotional articles, and one Christian music book. He has also edited two Christian magazines. He is a pastor, evangelist, musician, teacher, and father of six.

To see more of this author's work, go to http://faithwriters.com/testimonies2.php

SOMETHING BEAUTIFUL, SOMETHING GOOD
By Tim Pickl

My brother Terry always had a sly brotherly way of talking me into things. One night about twenty years ago, he wore a big, confident smile. "Hey brother, why don't you come to the Bible study with me tonight?"

This time it was something good. I really didn't have much else to do, I was interested, and Terry knew it, so I agreed. "Okay, sure, why not?"

Over the course of several weeks, we met, and we studied, learning the ways of God from His Word. I relearned many things from my childhood and things I'd never been taught. The Holy Ghost led us into all truth during our study, including the need to be baptized.

I'll never forget the night we studied Acts Chapter 2. We got down to the heart of the chapter—the keys of the kingdom of God that Peter received and preached—and Terry read it for all of us to hear. *"Then Peter said unto them, Repent, and be baptized every one of you in the name of Jesus Christ for the remission of sins, and ye shall receive the gift of the Holy Ghost. For the promise is unto you, and to your children, and to all that are afar off, even as many as the Lord our God shall call." (Acts 2:38-39 KJV)*

I jumped up and excitedly exclaimed, "That's in the Bible? I can't believe it. Wow!"

Our friend, who was teaching the Bible study, smiled and gently said, "Terry, go ahead and read it again."

He did, our friend explained baptism, and I immediately wanted to be baptized. But we waited until that Sunday night—the last Sunday in June 1987. I was nervous, excited, and serious. It was "the most important day of my life," my Pastor said, and I felt like I was getting married. (Later that year, I learned that I'd joined the bride of Christ, by taking on His Name—Jesus.)

The church people gathered around the baptismal tank; some were singing and playing a song, while others were praising and thanking God and praying. It was a joyful sound.

I stepped down into the water and turned around. My pastor prayed with me before he baptized me, "In the Name of Jesus Christ for the remission of sins." He laid me back into the water, and buried me, and suddenly:

All was quiet.

The sounds of the singing and praising and praying were immediately muffled.

> *"Know ye not, that so many of us as were baptized into Jesus Christ were baptized into his death? Therefore we are buried with him by baptism into death: that like as Christ was raised up from the dead by the glory of the Father, even so we also should walk in newness of life." (Romans 6:3-4 KJV)*

It was a moment when the eternity of Heaven intersected with the present, as the blood of Jesus washed my sins away. When I came up out of that water all I could think and feel was, *Wow! I have never felt so clean—on the inside.*

I heard the singing and praising again, and I praised God right with them. I raised my hands as tears of joy mixed with water streamed down my face, and I spoke in other tongues as the Spirit of God gave the utterance.

Jesus found me. He delivered me and saved me from my sins; I don't have to submit myself to alcohol, or drugs, or lying or stealing. Praise God. This scripture became true in my life: *"Jesus answered, 'Verily, verily, I say unto thee, except a man be born of water and of the Spirit, he cannot enter into the kingdom of God.'" (John 3:5 KJV)*

Several days later, I was sitting in the back of the sanctuary at the Family Church Campgrounds. It was my birthday, and the sun was shining on my back. A small group was practicing songs for the evening service, and one of the songs by Bill and Gloria Gaither, "Something Beautiful," was so appropriate, just for me, right then.

I bent forward, weeping. Several wonderful brothers and sisters gathered around me and prayed for me. Such love, such compassion, such caring. I still cry.

ABOUT THE AUTHOR

Tim Pickl is a loving husband, father, guardian and grandpa from Hartland, Wisconsin. He is a webmaster for his church and author of short stories, poems and plays to the glory of God. To see more of this author's work, go to http://faithwriters.com/testimonies2.php.

EPILOGUE

Rooted and Grounded in God's Love

As we have seen, the authors in this book do not have perfect lives. They actually have something much better, a heartfelt understanding of the most important thing, a correct awareness that God does love them. Looking away from life's ever-changing circumstances that we will all face to some degree, they keep their eyes focused on the unchanging truth of God's love seen in Jesus' sacrifice on the cross. They know and believe the love that God has for them (1 John 4:16*). When they read Jesus' words in John 17:23 that "… *so that the world may know that you sent me and loved them even as you loved me,*" they simply believe Jesus. They do not allow anything, especially circumstances, to diminish the truth of these very clear Bible verses. The knowledge of their Father's personal love for them is vital in their ability to move forward and keep the faith, no matter what life brings.

When people are truly rooted and grounded in God's love for them, they trust God totally; their lives are transformed, and the peace that surpasses all understanding promised by Jesus is produced as a fruit in their lives (Philippians 4:7). This peace only comes when they look away from themselves, and instead, look completely unto Jesus' obedience on the cross. They realize their salvation has nothing to do with themselves in the past, present, or future and everything to do with Jesus. This peace, no matter what happens, is one of the greatest blessings that extends to and beyond present circumstances to all other struggles, including death, that are certain to come in this life.

Do You *Know* That God Loves You Regardless of Your Sins?

I don't mean just the words and head knowledge. I mean, do you know and believe in your heart that God really loves you and wants the best for you? This is true, whether you are currently trusting in him or not, as John 3:16 states, *"For God so loved the world, that he gave his only Son, that **whoever** believes in him should not perish but have eternal life,"*

Are you focused on your circumstances, worried, and fearful about what eternity might hold for you? Just as the writers of this book know how much God loves them, I am here to tell you that you, too, can know for yourself exactly how much God loves you. You can experience the absolute knowledge of your salvation for eternity and the peace that surpasses all circumstances. It all starts with an intimate knowledge of God's perfect personal love for you. This knowledge will transform your life and his perfect love will cast out all fear (1 John 4:18). God the Father wants to be your Father. He yearns to have a loving personal relationship with you.

How You Can Know and Believe That God Loves and Wants the Best for You?

"So we have come to know and to believe the love that God has for us. God is love, and whoever abides in love abides in God, and God abides in him." (1 John 4:16)

The best way to know and believe how much God loves you and what he wants for you is to study Jesus' actions and words. The Bible states in Hebrews 1:3 that *"He [Jesus] is the radiance of the glory of God and the exact imprint of his nature.*" When Jesus, full of love and compassion for the lost, was asked to show people the Father, he replied, *"If you had known me, you would have known my Father also. From now on you do know him and have seen him"* (*John 14:7*).

When we study Jesus' actions and words, we find that he was always compassionate and loving to all, even the worst of sinners. We see it particularly in his attitude to his disciples; no matter how often they fell short, he never condemned them. His ministry was one of reconciling the lost to God the Father. The worst of the worst would hide from the religious leaders, but they would flock to Jesus. They saw his compassion, lack of judgment, and love for them. *"... For whatever the Father does, that the Son does likewise." (John 5:19)*

We can see the obvious love, compassion, and the Father's nature displayed in Jesus' actions in many Biblical stories, including that of John 8:1-11, in which a woman who had been caught in the very act of adultery was dragged before Jesus. In an attempt to discredit Jesus by enforcing the letter of the law, the religious leaders wanted to stone the woman as the law required. However, Jesus pointed out to them that only a person with no sin had the right to judge and condemn another person. Even though they caught the woman in the very act and she was obviously guilty, when hit with the reality that they were just as guilty before God as the woman, they could doing nothing but drop their stones and walk away. This is an important truth, and it tells us that the only one who can judge us is God himself.

Many readers miss an interesting and important fact in this passage. There was one person there who was sinless and could judge, condemn her, and cast a stone–Jesus himself, the exact imprint of God the Father's nature (Hebrews 1:3). As the sinless Son of God, he could have picked up a stone and cast it at the woman. Likewise, he could also condemn you and me for our multitude of sins, but that is not what Jesus desires to do. He told her, as he is telling you, that he does not condemn her or you. In that case, the specified sin was adultery, but you can place yourself along with any one of your sins (yes, my friend, any sin) in the story, and Jesus would have reacted the exact same way. John 3:17 says, *"For God did not send his Son into the world to condemn the world, but in order that the world might be saved through him."* Repeatedly, in Jesus, we see the Father's true heart towards us. 1 Timothy 2:3-4 reaffirms Jesus's love for us. *"This is good, and it is pleasing in the sight of God our Savior, who desires all people to be saved and to come to the knowledge of the truth."*

Are You The Prodigal Child?

For many, it is easy to see that Jesus loves and feels compassion for sinners, but they do not view the Father in the same way. Honestly, this breaks God the Father's heart; he sent Jesus to save us because he loves us. *"For **God so loved the world**, that he gave his only Son, that whoever believes in him should not perish but have eternal life. (John 3:16)* Yet many glance over the words, *"God so loved the world,"* and don't fully comprehend that is the reason why Jesus came to the world as the Savior. The sad truth is that many will never trust God enough to follow his simple directions to be saved because they have been deceived into thinking God does not love them or that God is out to get them.

When confronted with the false belief that some are beyond God's love and salvation, Jesus himself gives a description of God the Father's true nature in the parable (a simple story used to illustrate a moral or spiritual lesson) of the prodigal son. In it, Jesus dispels the lie that God does not love us and is out to punish us. This parable clearly reveals the Father's unconditional love for any person who has rejected him and lived in **sin and unbelief.** As you read the following parable and commentary, place yourself in the position of the rebellious, younger son.

The Prodigal Son, Luke 15:11-24

"¹¹And he said, "There was a man who had two sons. ¹²And the younger of them said to his father, 'Father, give me the share of property that is coming to me.' And he divided his property between them. ¹³Not many days later, the younger son gathered all he had and took a journey into a far country, and there he squandered his property in reckless living"

The parable started out with the younger son (a picture of you) asking for his inheritance from his father (God), so that he could leave and go his own way. It is important to note the level of rejection the son expresses towards his father at this point. It is the picture of how many of us have rejected God to go our own way. Normally, the son would be required to wait for his inheritance until his father had died. By making this request, the son is rejecting his father and the entire family; in essence, he is telling his father that he wished he were dead. Even though the request was highly unusual, the father agrees, and the son leaves and goes off to live life on his own terms, forgetting about his father for a time.

"¹⁴And when he had spent everything, a severe famine arose in that country, and he began to be in need. ¹⁵So he went and hired himself out to one of the citizens of that country, who sent him into his fields to feed pigs. ¹⁶And he was longing to be fed with the pods that the pigs ate, and no one gave him anything."

In verses 14-16, we see that that the son's trust in money, his own ability, and wisdom has let him down. He ends up living in the ruins of his lifestyle, as many of us do. He is wallowing in the mud, feeding pigs, and longing for food but has none.

"[17]*But when he came to himself, he said, 'How many of my father's hired servants have more than enough bread, but I perish here with hunger!* [18]*I will arise and go to my father, and I will say to him, "Father, I have sinned against heaven and before you.* [19]*I am no longer worthy to be called your son. Treat me as one of your hired servants."*

In verses 17-19, we see the son is broke, destitute, and at the bottom of the barrel. He comes to his senses and admits to himself that he has really messed up and hurt his father. This change of mind (repentance) leads him to return to his father (describes our return to God), even though he fears and anticipates some level of judgment. So, just in case, he decides to offer to be a servant in his father's home in order to appease him. He even rehearses what he will say to soothe his father's anticipated anger.

"[20a] *and he arose and came to his father."*

Unbeknownst to the son, the father, who the son had rejected and scorned, had been watching and hoping for his son's return. Jesus tells us that the son (representing any lost soul who returns to the Father) is in for a huge surprise.

"[20b] *But while he was still a long way off, his father saw him and felt compassion, and ran and embraced him and kissed him.* [21]*And the son said to him, 'Father, I have sinned against heaven and before you. I am no longer worthy to be called your son.'* [22]*But the father said to his servants, 'Bring quickly the best robe, and put it on him, and put a ring on his hand, and shoes on his feet.* [23]*And bring the fattened calf and kill it, and let us eat and celebrate.* [24]*For this my son was dead, and is alive again; he was lost, and is found.' And they began to celebrate."*

Amazingly, Jesus tells us that the father (God), who had been rejected and had endured his son (you) doing the opposite of what he wanted him to do, does not judge, condemn, or punish his child at all. On the contrary, he welcomes him home with open arms, incredible compassion, and a huge celebration.

While this may be contrary to your current belief, what you have just read is Jesus' personal description of God's love for **you**. Jesus, himself, is telling you that compassion, love, acceptance, blessing, forgiveness for your sins, and eternal life are what awaits you. Even though you do not have all the answers, you just need to take God at his word, trust Jesus, and come home to your Father who is patiently waiting to express his love to you, tell you your debt has been paid, and to give to you his gift of forgiveness.

God Loves You

"For God so loved the world, that he gave his only Son, that whoever believes in him should not perish but have eternal life." (John 3:16)

***But** God shows his love for us in that while we were still sinners, Christ died for us." (Romans 5:8)*

All Are Sinners

"...for all have sinned and fall short of the glory of God." (Romans 3:23)

"None is righteous, no, not one." (Romans 3:10)

God's Remedy for Sin

"For the wages of sin is death, but the free gift of God is eternal life in Christ Jesus our Lord." (Romans 6:23)

"But to all who did receive him, who believed in his name, he gave the right to become children of God." (John 1:12)

All May Be Saved Now

"For everyone who calls on the name of the Lord will be saved." (Romans 10:13)

"...but these are written so that you may believe that Jesus is the Christ, the Son of God, and that by believing you may have life in his name." (John 20:31)

Come home, prodigal child, by receiving Christ as your Savior now. While specific words are not as important as your heart's attitude, we offer you this simple prayer to use:

"Father, I admit I am a sinner and my past lack of trust in you and your promise. I now repent and change my mind from unbelief to belief. I take you at your word and believe that Jesus died for my sins on the cross and was raised for my justification. I believe Jesus is who he claimed to be, God the Son in the flesh. I accept him as my personal Lord and Savior. I am willing to transformed by your Holy Spirit and pray your will, not mine, be done in my life. Amen."

Please visit our website for more information about your new life in Christ. You can also let us know about your decision and learn what to do next.
http://faithwritersjesuspage.weebly.com/new-believer-resources.html

BIBLE VERSES TO SHOW GOD LOVES YOU

Bible Verses to Help You Remain Rooted and Grounded in God's Love

So that Christ may dwell in your hearts through faith—that you, **being rooted and grounded in love,** *may have strength to comprehend with all the saints what is the breadth and length and height and depth, and to know the love of Christ that surpasses knowledge, that you may be filled with all the fullness of God. (Ephesians 3:17-19)*

"So we have come to know and to believe the love that God has for us. *God is love, and whoever abides in love abides in God, and God abides in him." (1 John 4:16)*

"I will forgive their iniquity, I will remember their sin no more." (Jeremiah 31:34b)

I in them and you in me, that they may become perfectly one, so that the world may know that you sent me and **loved them even as you loved me.** *(John 17:23)*

Just so, I tell you, there will be more joy in heaven over one sinner who repents than over ninety-nine righteous persons who need no repentance. (Luke 15:7)

As the Father has loved me, so have I loved you. Abide in my love. (John 15:9)

We love because he first loved us. (1 John 4:19)

In this is love, not that we have loved God but that he loved us and sent his Son to be the propitiation for our sins. (1 John 4:10)

Who shall separate us from the love of Christ? Shall tribulation, or distress, or persecution, or famine, or nakedness, or danger, or sword? As it is written, "For your sake we are being killed all the day long; we are regarded as sheep to be slaughtered." No, in all these things we are more than conquerors through him who loved us. For I am sure that neither death nor life, nor angels nor rulers, nor things present nor things to come, nor powers, nor height nor depth, nor anything else in all creation, will be able to separate us from the love of God in Christ Jesus our Lord. (Romans 8:35-39)

But God shows his love for us in that while we were still sinners, Christ died for us. (Romans 5:8)

"For God so loved the world, that he gave his only Son, that whoever believes in him should not perish but have eternal life. (John 3:16)

The Lord appeared to him from far away. I have loved you with an everlasting love; therefore I have continued my faithfulness to you. (Jeremiah 31:3)

See what kind of love the Father has given to us, that we should be called children of God; and so we are. The reason why the world does not know us is that it did not know him. (1 John 3:1)

I have been crucified with Christ. It is no longer I who live, but Christ who lives in me. And the life I now live in the flesh I live by faith in the Son of God, who loved me and gave himself for me. (Galatians 2:20)

In this the love of God was made manifest among us, that God sent his only Son into the world, so that we might live through him. (1 John 4:9)

Anyone who does not love does not know God, because God is love. (1 John 4:8)

Greater love has no one than this, that someone lay down his life for his friends. (John 15:13)

By this we know love, that he laid down his life for us, and we ought to lay down our lives for the brothers. (1 John 3:16)

So now faith, hope, and love abide, these three; but the greatest of these is love. (1 Corinthians 13:13)

If I give away all I have, and if I deliver up my body to be burned, but have not love, I gain nothing. Love is patient and kind; love does not envy or boast; it is not arrogant or rude. It does not insist on its own way; it is not irritable or resentful; it does not rejoice at wrongdoing, but rejoices with the truth. Love bears all things, believes all things, hopes all things, endures all things. (1 Corinthians 13:3-10)

For I know the plans I have for you, declares the Lord, plans for welfare and not for evil, to give you a future and a hope. (Jeremiah 29:11)

Keep your life free from love of money, and be content with what you have, for he has said, "I will never leave you nor forsake you." (Hebrews 13:5)

For the love of Christ controls us, because we have concluded this: that one has died for all, therefore all have died; (2 Corinthians 5:14)

As far as the east is from the west, so far does he remove our transgressions from us. (Psalm 103:12)

Because your steadfast love is better than life, my lips will praise you. (Psalm 63:3)

For I, the Lord your God, hold your right hand; it is I who say to you, "Fear not, I am the one who helps you." (Isaiah 41:13)[*]

---

[*] All verses above are from the English Standard Version ® (ESV®) of the Holy Bible.